Sierra Vista

Young City with a Past

Bayleaf is surrounded by his friends. He was the first dog working for the Sierra Vista Department of Public Safety. (Courtesy of the Henry Hauser Museum.)

Dedication

To Ron: "Thank you" from the bottom of my heart, for your months of understanding, for cups of hot tea, for running errands, for all the times you'd speak and I (living somewhere in the past) would say, "Huh?" You are my rock!

THE
MAKING OF AMERICA
SERIES

SIERRA VISTA

YOUNG CITY WITH A PAST

ETHEL JACKSON PRICE

ISBN 978-1-58973-065-6

Published by Arcadia Publishing
Charleston SC, Chicago IL, Portsmouth NH, San Francisco CA

For all general information contact Arcadia Publishing at:
Telephone 843-853-2070
Fax 843-853-0044
E-Mail sales@arcadiapublishing.com
For customer service and orders:
Toll-Free 1-888-313-2665

Visit us on the Internet at www.arcadiapublishing.com.

Front cover: *At the crossroads (left to right) are Buster Pyeatt, Jim Pyeatt, and Ronnie Pyeatt. The two boys are Buster's sons; Ronnie currently operates a feed store in Huachuca City. The lady is Rose Pyeatt. The young boy in front is Teddy Hale, a family friend. (Identified by Ronnie Pyeatt; photo courtesy of Kathy Mayo.)*

Contents

ACKNOWLEDGMENTS

I could not have written this story of Sierra Vista, Arizona without the help of some great people. Who are (or were) they? They're the adventurers, miners, soldiers, ranchers, frontierswomen, and Apaches who inhabit these pages. They're an active part of it all. I'm honored by the privilege of walking the same ground and breathing the same air.

Then there's my all-volunteer research team who made phone calls, suggested many a "go-see," offered pictures or information, and who, many times, trusted me with intrinsically valuable collections of old newspapers, documents, and more. To them, I offer my undying appreciation.

I would like to thank Marisa Fusco for first suggesting that I do this book—then backing it up with pictures and clippings from the Henry Hauser Museum. Others on my "Appreciation List" are Jim Finley, Joyce Rowand, Cyndi Padgette, Cliff Brown, Mary Estes, the late author Norine Haverty Dickey, and all my fellow members of the museum and Historical Committee.

Ricardo Alonzo, a resident of Sierra Vista and a terrific artist, gave most generously of his time and talent to help readers "see" buildings no longer here; let us all say thanks the next time we see him.

A special note of appreciation goes to Kathy Mayo for all the legwork, phone calls, etc. I'm looking forward to working with Kathy again soon. Indeed, I must recognize all my research assistants, a.k.a. "The Landmark Gang:" besides Kathy, they are Kay Mayo, Marie Storment, Nola Walker, Nola's daughter Charlotte and son David, Paul Knoles, Jan Knoles, and more. I am truly honored to call each of you my friend.

I also owe a debt of gratitude to the *Sierra Vista Herald* and to Pat Wick, who gave me access to the *Herald's* "morgue," thereby both fanning and feeding my appetite for the community's history, and for granting permission to use the files as a major source of information and documentation.

Last but not least, I want to offer my deepest appreciation to Arcadia Publishing and to Jim Kempert (my editor) for tolerating the occasional panic attack, cranky moods, unexpected delays so crazy that no one could make them up, and for once telling me to take some time off, to go see a movie or something. Jim, don't ever quit your job; we need you!

INTRODUCTION

Silver. Gold. Copper. Cows. Strangely, considering that we have no mines or smelters in Sierra Vista proper, these things are why we're in this particular corner of Cochise County. Ranches are not in the city, but they're very close by. There are caves nearby, of course, including one with a story as wild as that of The Lost Dutchman Mine you will read later, but mines, both famous and infamous, and smelters, etc.? They've never existed here, only in locations that probably qualify (using today's standards) as "nearby." Still, Tombstone silver, Bisbee copper, and a smattering of gold here and there have a lot to do with this community's history. So does cattle. In the late nineteenth century, this was ranchland with a few small settlements here and there. Cattle means ranches; ranches need cowboys; cowboys often begin a family; families require support services; those providing the services often become a community; communities grow. (For instance, Sierra Vista's population once increased by more than 10,000 overnight—due to an event that had nothing to do with mining or ranching!)

Unincorporated until 1956, this city is, comparatively speaking, young, but its very youth is quite a plus. Its people are mostly energetic and ambitious with a vision of the city's future. Has it been a struggle? Sometimes. There are always a few who want things to stay the way they've always been, not realizing that things either go forward or back but never stay the same. Fortunately, city fathers persevered; they've hauled Sierra Vista—often kicking and screaming—right straight into the twenty-first century.

It's actually quite fitting that Sierra Vista is in Arizona; after all, Arizona—the last of the 48 contiguous states—is somewhat of an upstart itself, less than 100 years old as a state. That doesn't mean the area was non-existent, or even uninhabited, before it was the State of Arizona. Unfortunately, there are learned people who claim Sierra Vista has little history, no cultural resources, and no real background. Not so! It all depends on how one defines history, culture, and background.

Seemingly tucked neatly away, surrounded and protected by several mountain ranges, the city is separate from the more familiar Santa Cruz corridor. Many historians would have you believe that the whole of Arizona's essence is tied especially to the Santa Cruz riverbank, but it isn't. This particular corner survived the Spanish conquerors' often cruel search for gold and much of their (sometimes equally as cruel) religious colonization. It lasted through the Indian Wars (a horrible tragedy for both sides), at least one incredibly devastating earthquake, and some forest fires. Today, it's dealing with a highly controversial situation little understood in other parts of the country: the nearly overwhelming influx of illegal immigrants. Still, this corner of Arizona—where a nearby community calls itself "the town too tough to die"—survives. It will continue to survive.

Perhaps one thing affecting Sierra Vista's perceived history is that early maps, depending on their purpose, often show different territorial lines. One small spot could be labeled several different ways. The fact is, Sierra Vista is truly a border town close to the U.S. international border with Mexico. Our thrice-changed county line (another border) is now located just west of Fort Huachuca, a military reservation standing between the city and the next county line. In addition to all that, Sierra Vista is located barely 7 miles west of the San Pedro River, where, according to older maps, Pimeria Alta and Apacheria are said to meet. Looking at other maps and drawing intersecting lines, one finds that Cochise County is obviously right square in the middle of Apacheria. Yes, in today's parlance, such a place might be called "No Man's Land."

The fact is, early explorers' obsession with lines of demarcation often meant they claimed territory based on landmarks, such as everything between the San Pedro River and the Santa Cruz River. Therefore, simply because a couple of

This old tree by San Pedro House, right next to the San Pedro River that forms the western border of Apacheria, is about 7 miles from Sierra Vista. The visitor remains unidentified. (Courtesy of Brendan Earle.)

Spanish explorers made separate trips on two different rivers, old maps show the exact spot where downtown Sierra Vista now exists as being within Pimeria Alta. Practically speaking, it isn't, although one could ask "Where are we?" or "Who are we?" You see, this southwest corner of Cochise Country was, in addition to being the home of more than one Indian nation, once part of Sonora, Mexico. Later, it was part of New Mexico, then one of Arizona Territory's four original counties. Another time, it was no less than an official part of the Confederacy, subject to the Stars and Bars by presidential decree.

All that is mere background, things that happened before Sierra Vista existed. The city began its own life as two homesteads outside the perimeters of an army post, homesteads that grew into a "stringtown" and absorbed other small communities. Before incorporation, this community went through several name changes. I've discovered eight names, including one that's quite literally colorful. The name "Fry" (not spelled with an 'e', as some historians would have it) was considered at the time of incorporation. Sadly, a local joke about why Fry was not selected is often repeated as gospel truth. Records will finally be set straight herein, and we'll meet the Sierra Vistan who caused the city to bear its official name. And we'll learn how her action affected city boundaries.

Today, the nearby military post has a substantial economic impact on the city, but Sierra Vista has survived its two closures. Having done so, the city enjoys a uniquely symbiotic relationship with Fort Huachuca where a portion of the original construction has become historically significant. The site of numerous archeological digs and more, the post remains an active, working facility, while others created during the Apache Wars were abandoned long, long ago.

A number of civilians are employed at the post. It's a trade. Fort Huachuca's soldiers, many of whom today live and shop in Sierra Vista, have gone from itchy wool uniforms in Cavalry-blue to lightweight, appropriately-mottled "Battle Dress Uniforms" (BDUs), from heliographs to state-of-the-art computer technology, from riding horses to driving Humvees. And its soldiers, men and women, continue marching alongside Sierra Vista straight into and through the twenty-first century, making history along the way.

NOTE: Descendants of the Apache warrior Geronimo still live in Cochise County and have loaned materials to the museum. They have, however, asked that their names not be revealed; both the museum and I have promised to honor their request and, therefore, their more recent history is not discussed herein.

1. Influence of the Spanish Crown

A shipwreck is ultimately the reason why Sierra Vista exists today. In 1528, a Spaniard named Alvar Nunez Cabeza de Vaca survived a shipwreck off the southeast coast of Texas. Most of his shipmates and whatever cargo was being transported—possibly cattle, as his name would loosely indicate—were lost. Cabeza de Vaca and a few friends, battered though they were, either swam ashore or washed in on the tide. Either way, four men eventually found themselves resting on sand. Hot sun dried their clothing. Nothing was broken or scraped that wouldn't heal. Things were bad, but at least they were still alive. They'd have to find shelter and food, of course, but such tasks were manageable. Unfortunately, they didn't enjoy the beach for long.

Captured almost immediately by Native Americans, Nunez and three of his companions spent some time as prisoners before eventually managing to escape. For the next eight years, they struggled on foot, finding their way back to civilization in Mexico City. Once they had returned, stories from Cabeza de Vaca's imagination—perhaps fueled during those eight years in the jungle—became mixed with Spanish legends about Seven Cities of Gold and even wilder stories told by the Native Americans. Spurred on by his reception as a survivor, he embroidered his stories still further. He soon told of wonderful riches to be found in the vast, uncharted lands north of the path he'd traveled. Cabeza de Vaca's stories soon caught the attention of government rulers.

Under orders subsequently issued by the viceroy of Mexico, Fray Marcos de Niza mounted an expedition that brought him into what is now San Pedro River territory in the late spring of 1539. Fateful events, including the death of his guide, caused de Niza to greatly fear entering even the first small city believed to be part of Cibola (the so-called 'Seven Cities of Gold'). He returned to Mexico where, for reasons of pride or whatever, he found himself telling made-up stories not necessarily of Cibola but of incredible riches just waiting for discovery.

Within a year, armor glinted in the bright sunlight and plumes danced atop the officers' helmets. There were over 200 conquistadores on horseback, some 60-plus foot soldiers, with enough workers and servants to bring the numbers

Struggling to reach what is now called Montezuma Pass in the Huachuca Mountains, the leader and his complete entourage looked back to where they'd been. Nearby is Coronado Peak (elevation 6,864 feet), Montezuma Peak (elevation 7,676 feet), and more. Though now in Arizona, the pass was then in Sonora; that's Mexico in the distance.

to around 1,000 people, plus over 1,500 heads of livestock intended for either transportation or food. Spanish foot soldiers left Mexico in layered leather gear, sweating in the heat as they toiled up and over Montezuma Pass. The expedition was under the command of Francisco Vasquez de Coronado (1510–1554), who'd settled in Mexico after arriving from Spain when he was just 25 years old.

After marrying and starting a family, Coronado had been appointed governor of the province of Nueva Galicia before being tempted by the stories of the Seven Cities of Gold. He mounted a well-equipped (for the times) but ill-fated expedition to find those cities. In their search, they marched generally northward into new and unexplored territory that they claimed for Spain.

The conquerors could not imagine that native peoples were anything other than uncivilized. The land, therefore, was all available to he who first laid claim.

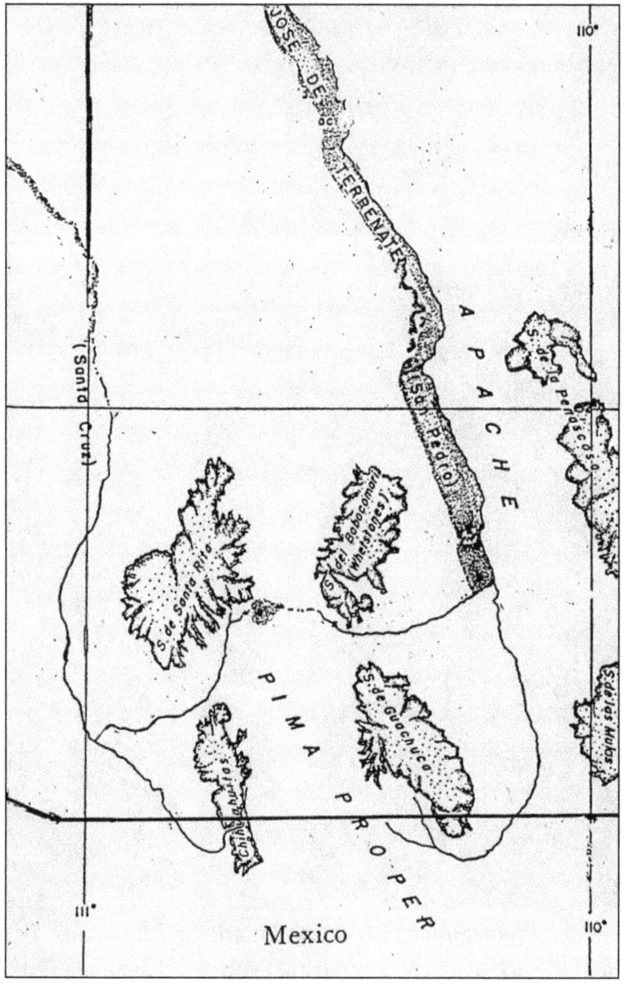

This map shows the proximity of the Santa Cruz River, forming the Santa Cruz Corridor leading northward, and the San Pedro River, which is pertinent to Apacheria and the future Sierra Vista. The rivers' headwaters are in Mexico. Lower San Pedro is actually northward, closer to where it joins the Gila River (once Mexico's northern border). Note the Spanish spelling of some names such as "S. de Guachuca," which translates to Huachuca Mountains. (Courtesy of Rosario Guzman.)

Already, entire regions had been mapped out, lines drawn, Spanish names—not Indian names—given to rivers, mountains, communities, etc.

These good-intentioned groups had been given a huge assignment: find the celebrated Cities of Gold and, along the way, colonize. And introduce Christianity to the native peoples (a duty added when an earlier explorer found that many Indian men not only drank too much but had several wives). Consequently, groups usually included not only the soldiers but zealous volunteers who, along with teaching a new religion that disallowed heavy drinking and multiple wives, were expected to spread the Spanish language and Spanish customs.

Somehow, it never occurred to any of them that they were invading, not discovering. The general expectation was that the Crown's version of civilization, defined as being "under Spanish influence and guidance," would cause all the assorted Indian nations to lay down their arms. They would give up fighting with each other, give up raids on enemy villages, give up freedom and autonomy. With proper guidance, they would all become wonderfully docile, peace-loving (and tax-paying, of course) servants of the Spanish crown.

Thus, to accomplish such ambitious plans, missionaries were included on many an exploration. As they spread their faith, they built a series of protective missions, usually along riverbanks. These settlements followed a mostly northward pattern from New Spain, through Sonora and present-day Nogales, on up the Santa Cruz River to what is now Phoenix, and beyond. Historians tend to dwell on that area while ignoring this side of the mountains.

Of note, however, is that when missions were built, they weren't really for the soldiers and not entirely for the religious leaders. It was all because Spain's eyes were fixed on the money. Money and control, which would bring even more money when the native peoples were taught to respect their masters and to be humbly grateful for what Spain was doing for them, made the missions necessary.

It began with a bunch of poppycock when a respected explorer took word back to the Crown that he'd seen entire villages made of gold. Spain wanted that gold. Thus, the report spawned a series of ill-conceived, explorational searches for those villages. Eventually, Cibola (a.k.a. the Seven Cities of Gold) were discovered to be nothing more than bright sun reflected off adobe huts, and interest certainly waned. However, it wasn't long until the dream resurfaced in different form.

In their earlier searches, explorers noted but passed by signs of rich mineral deposits in the north. They saw evidence of silver and copper and, yes, some gold; it just wasn't the Seven Cities. They did, however, report the sightings. When word eventually filtered back to Spain, it piqued the Crown's interest and created new visions of fabulous wealth through colonization. So, in a first come, first served manner, the Spaniards came.

Of course, once walled missions were in place, communities grew around them. Gardens were planted and the daily business of life went on. Along the Santa Cruz corridor, members of several Indian villages were arguably converted to the strange new faith (though scholars may question whether they stayed "converted" or not) and, for protection from their enemies, brought more families into the fold. Sometimes the missions weren't enough. To protect settlers and missions from rampaging Indians and from bandits, actual forts—called presidios (such as early Tucson)—were built. They were effective. Expansion continued in a somewhat steady northward pattern geared to the Santa Cruz River and its tributaries. It is an area entirely west of today's Cochise County.

Eventually, needing to refresh their funds and their treasury, the Spanish Crown decided to make use of the minerals found during their search for the Seven Cities. To get them out of the ground, they needed miners, lots of miners. Recruitment (and rumors) spread; soon, willing miners began arriving from all parts of the world. It wasn't long until even the comparatively peaceful O'odham became restive, apprehensive at the sheer, overwhelming number of arrogant foreigners pouring into their homeland, foreigners who considered the Native Americans uncivilized and treated them as such.

Adding to their frustration, the O'odham were no longer free, no longer in control of their own lives; they had been forcibly taken over and just as forcibly coerced to help dig deep into their own earth. But for what? They gained nothing from it. Their unbelievably backbreaking labor produced something that brought them no deliverance. It simply disappeared. The food they were given wasn't what they had eaten for centuries, not what their systems demanded. They were not fed well at all but were subject to beatings at the overseer's slightest whim. Suffering what amounted to slave labor, the Indians saw everything they produced going to the invaders or the invaders' overseas government. The rumbling swell of discontent grew louder; soon, a group of O'odham mounted a bloody but doomed revolt. The superior organization, sheer numbers, and advanced weaponry of the Spanish soon ended the action.

To the invaders, such ongoing rebellions were a manageable problem. Because most Indian groups considered each village to be separate and independent as its own nation, their uprisings were, generally speaking, not a coalition of organized groups in a systematic confrontation. Instead, such rebellions were usually isolated events taking place within a somewhat loose perimeter, this group against that particular presidio. They warred against the individual settlement, but not against the Spanish as a whole.

In the meantime, word continued to spread. As often "embroidered" stories reached European shores, interest grew. Such tales! Governments and powerful kings and queens were told of fabulous, but unlimited and untapped, riches just waiting to be retrieved. France and England especially were fast becoming more and more interested in New Spain. Their coffers needed money. Money—and new land—was power. Wanting their own large slice of the pie, they started moving in. Spain felt the squeeze. To keep a firm hold on what they now considered their territory, Spain added additional military reinforcements to missions and to presidios originally intended only to protect settlers from the Native Americans. Soldiers are soldiers, not farmers or gatherers; therefore, more soldiers meant more civilian support was needed. The civilians needed soldiers for protection. The cycle went around and around.

Soldiers stationed in the presidios were, of course, charged with protecting not only the individuals within their walls, but also the farmers, ranchers, and miners working outside the walls. The troops found themselves spread thin, fighting on several fronts at once. It meant involvement with the O'odham as well as with a group more accustomed to ferocious guerrilla-type fighting: the Apaches, a tribe also of the firm opinion that their home territory was being stolen from them. Though they often raided other Indian nations, none involved were of a mind to let the "White Eyes" do the same thing. It would, they thought, be possible to drive out the strange invaders from their settlements.

For what would become Arizona, judging from old maps, most settlements were established along the Santa Cruz River and its tributaries. Somehow, the San Pedro was discovered, explored, and named as the eastern boundary of Pimeria Alta, but escaped the development and zealous mission-building of the near west. Perhaps the ferociousness of the Apaches had something to do with it.

The Spanish certainly had their problems. Not only was there France and England to deal with, but there was an upstart nation called the United States on the East Coast. Its citizens were a restless, ambitious, adventuresome lot, and seeing anything west of their territory as unsettled open space, they were already pushing toward the sunset.

One thing was certain. With increased settlement, with families moving in from Europe and Mexico and, soon, the East, more and more food was needed. Unlike individuals, communities of whatever size soon discovered that private hunting or fishing were not enough. Diets were substantially different than they are now, and the people needed meat in large quantities. Men wise in such things looked around and discovered that Sonora was perfect for growing cattle. There was plenty of open space, good weather, clear streams of running water, and a wonderful abundance of grass that sometimes grew as high as a horse's shoulder. It wasn't long till huge ranches of thousands and thousands of acres each developed, supplying beef not only to the Mexicans but to cities in the increasingly-populated eastern United States.

Times had been and still were turbulent. Mexico gained a hard-won independence from Spain in 1822; however, by so doing, it assumed responsibility for controlling

This archaelogical dig at Garden Canyon Project on Fort Huachuca by the University of Arizona investigates indigenous peoples. Fire and vandals caused some damage, and now it is covered over and restored to its former state not visible to the ordinary visitor. (Courtesy of Ron Price.)

all the Indian troubles within its perimeter. Somewhat unfortunately, that included what is now Cochise County. Next, in 1824, the Mexican government combined Sonora and Sinaloa to form a new state called Occidente. No one is 100 percent sure, but Occidente might have gone north all the way to the Gila River. One thing we do know is that by 1830 it reverted to its former arrangement of the two separate towns. Occidente no longer existed, and by 1831, the area where Sierra Vista now exists was an official part of Sonora, Mexico.

Sonora was large, its vast expanse not only difficult but expensive to manage and nearly impossible to defend militarily. After all, it was still an isolated territory with relatively few, scattered people. Deciding resources could be more efficiently utilized elsewhere, Mexico soon pulled back its forces, leaving huge areas undefended. Adding to Mexico's problems, bitter religious clashes raged between the Jesuits and Franciscans, soon turning into their own war. Unable to settle their differences amicably, through negotiation, the two groups did physical battle with each other. The Jesuits came out the winner of this clash. When, in 1837, the Franciscans were actually thrown out of Mexico, no one was left to manage things. Even the beautiful missions along the Santa Cruz corridor were no longer maintained and nature took its toll. They quickly began falling into great disarray.

So although the area now called Cochise County was rather neglected by the missionaries and colonists, it may have been a good thing in many ways. Certainly, the deterioration of missions to the west and south was not greatly felt. On the other hand, travelers through and settlers in what would become southeast Arizona had their own growing set of problems.

The California gold rush of 1849 brought numerous travelers through early Arizona, often within sight of the Huachuca Mountains. Some stayed, finding what they believed was their true heart's desire among the majestic mountains that seemed to touch the sky and the fertile valleys with all the grass and water one could want. They built ranches and villages. They grew cattle. Some dug riches from the ground, often feeling another presence but ignoring it, even as their hackles rose on the back of their necks. Was it their imagination? No. They were being silently watched. And the watchers waited.

Somewhat quiet for several years when wagon trains and travelers on horseback merely passed through on the way to California, the Chiricahua Apaches had always been more militantly aggressive than the O'odham. Growing more and more agitated at an increasing number of trappers, miners, and ranchers, the Apaches interpreted the influx of settlers as a threat. They (correctly, as it turned out) understood that their way of life was threatened, their very homeland being stolen or destroyed.

2. Territory Sold by Mexico to the United States

The territory's boundaries were still uncertain; however, the Treaty of Guadalupe, in 1848, had awarded all the land north of the Gila River to the United States. There was, of course, some dispute about where the boundary should actually exist, so the United States and Mexico began a survey the same year gold was discovered in California. The rush was on! Easterners crossed the wide (and wild) ranges in covered wagons and on horseback. Some didn't make it and were buried along the trail. Some made it all the way to the goldfields. A few stopped in the vast unsettled regions east of California, establishing a tenuous foothold in what was actually volatile Indian country.

It seems to be a given that governments can't abide a territory not belonging to someone. There must be borders. Therefore, politics being what they are, the Compromise Act of 1850 officially established the Territory of New Mexico. Everything north of the Gila River was included; the lower part, where Sierra Vista is today, was still in Sonora, Mexico.

In the meantime, huge cattle ranches had already been established, but ranchers and their vaqueros still needed a way to ship product back east. Roundups, the stuff of cowboy legends, were held twice each year. The huge cattle drives that followed were hard miles (and months) long, through often unfriendly Indian country. They dealt not only with other humans, but with the elements; an electrical storm, for instance, could send the not-too-intelligent cattle into a stampede and if one animal dared to stumble, the others didn't stop. Drovers, therefore, would begin with a certain count, fully expecting that number to change as the weeks went on. Having to hold the long drives meant an automatic reduction in total numbers (of "beeves," as they were called) through raids or stampedes. Adding to the problem, surviving cattle always lost weight, thereby lowering their selling price.

What was needed was a new method of transport. Enter the railroads. Railroads were in their infancy and a few railheads existed, but they were few and far between. In addition, they stopped east of the huge southwestern ranches. If the rail lines were somehow extended coast-to-coast, the ambitious posited, not only could they handle the cattle shipments, but—since gold had already been discovered in California—they could also transport huge amounts of ore. On their way back, the railroads could bring new settlers to populate the West. Visionary tycoons wanted to build rail lines clear across the territory, all the way from the east coast to the Pacific Ocean. Gold and cattle would go east; on the return trip, families, adventurers, businessmen, teachers, etc., would load up their belongings and go west. Then it would all start over again. It could be done, they said.

The problem was deciding where to build it. When Lieutenant A.W. Whipple conducted a railroad survey in 1853 and 1854, he soon discovered that the best place to lay track to build railroads unfortunately wasn't in the United States nor even in its territories. The best place to lay track was in northern Mexico. Whipple discussed the matter with Jefferson Davis, then secretary of war. Davis liked the plan, favoring what he called the "southern route," and he knew just the man to push the idea through difficult government channels. James Gadsden (a tough railroad promoter from South Carolina) was appointed, at Secretary Davis's suggestion, to handle negotiations with Mexico.

Gadsden was successful, in large part, because the self-proclaimed dictator of Mexico, the handsome Antonio Lopez de Santa Ana (born in Mexico on February 21, 1794, and therefore not a real Spaniard), was in desperate need of money.

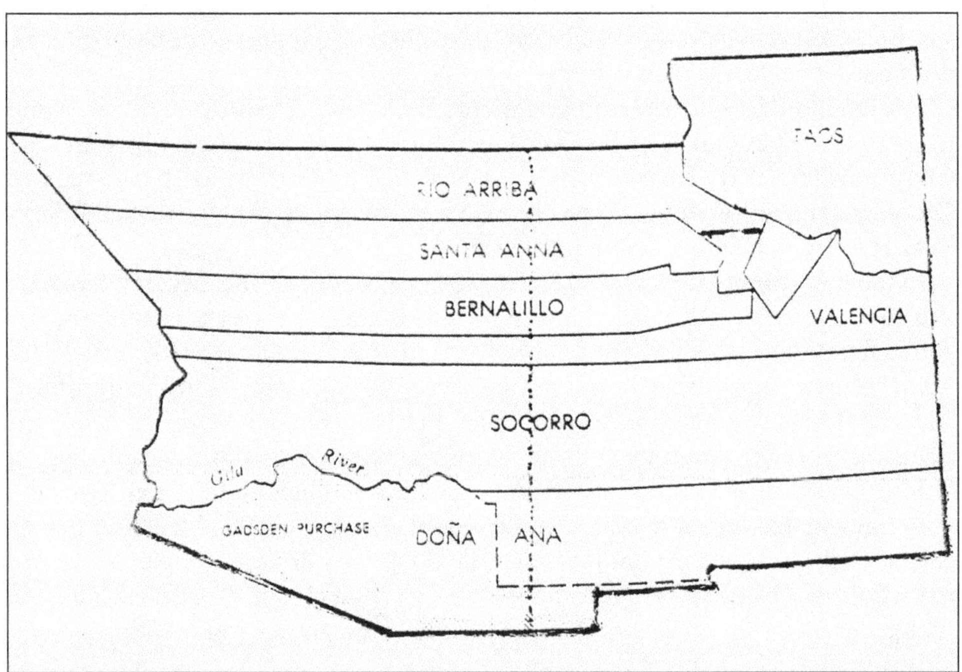

When the Territory of New Mexico was established, Arizona did not yet exist and the Gadsden Purchase (made because of railroad requirements) increased the size of the territory with counties as shown here. The perpendicular dotted line is the eventual border between the two territories. (Drawing courtesy of Steve Azevedo of Sonora, Mexico, age 12.)

Having first become a military officer at a young age, Santa Ana began by strongly supporting Emperor Agustin de Iturbide. He'd become infamous for attacking the Mission San Antonio de Valero (revered in Texas and later called "The Alamo"), before being captured at the Battle of San Jacinto. After his capture, he was unexpectedly allowed to return to Mexico, where he would later dominate Mexican politics.

After being legally appointed president of Mexico, the arrogant Santa Ana unilaterally decided the people of Mexico were "backward," uneducated, and unsophisticated; he believed they weren't ready for democracy and named himself dictator. The population dared not disagree—he was noted for his ruthless handling of such matters—which makes it difficult to believe that he was as popular with the peasantry as some claim. The truth is, they publicly proclaimed their admiration and respect for the dictator but secretly feared him.

Still, they talked among themselves and it wasn't long till word of the people's restless dissatisfaction reached Santa Ana. The problem was widespread, not just in the cities. As dictator, Santa Ana found himself embroiled in growing sedition within the borders of his own country.

Gadsden was more than pleased to discover that the new Mexican leader was fighting two fronts, that Santa Ana feared both an internal revolution and another war with the upstart United States. In fact, whether or not he had reason, he believed that the United States was going to annex all of Mexico. Was it true? Had the idea been deliberately planted and, if so, by whom? As with all good espionage, no one knows for sure. Regardless, Santa Ana knew there wasn't enough left in his treasury to fight another war against the United States, especially if it coincided with a rebellion within his own borders. He decided there was only one thing to do.

He swallowed some of his pride and strangely (though he'd gone to war to obtain freedom from them) turned to Spain for help. When Spain turned away his pleas, he tried France. Then England. All refused him. Desperately needing funds to keep his mismanaged regime together, but finally realizing that no European country was going to help, he capitulated. He decided to negotiate with Gadsden.

The president, taking advantage of the newly acquired intelligence, jumped on Gadsden's information about Santa Ana's predicament. Negotiations began, but it would not be as easy as anticipated. The United States wanted the border to continue straight west from Nogales. It wasn't just the miles or the acreage. While a straight line would be easier, and actually more beneficial to the United States, it would also physically divide Mexico into two parts; if the proposed border included a straight line going west from Nogales, there'd be no corridor connecting the main portion of Mexico to the peninsula now familiar as Baja California. Retaining its pride and digging in its heels, Mexico said "No." Proposals and counter-proposals flew back and forth. After five separate proposals and the several amendments that accompanied them, the men hammered out a deal allowing Mexico to keep a port on the Gulf of California along with a narrow land-bridge to it. Mexico, for their part, sold only a fragment of their territory to the United States for the specific purpose of building a new transcontinental railroad.

This new land was not captured in war and was not a colonization of new territory, but its purchase was (and sometimes still is) controversial in that some believe Santa Ana was trapped "between a rock and a hard place" and was unfairly coerced. Whether he was or not, he did hold strongly to one stipulation. He would sell only what the railroad needed. Whatever the economic coercion might have been, the basic purchase agreement was hammered out and both parties agreed to its terms. Only one item remained to be finalized. At the time of agreement, the new territorial border-to-be was somewhat tentative, not entirely fixed until later modification. When that item was finally decided, the line ran straight west from the Rio Grande, then took a sharp turn south and west through what is now Douglas, Arizona, to (loosely) Nogales. At that point, the plan changed from the original by veering northwest, putting the boundary exactly where it remains today.

The purchase also placed the new acquisition firmly in the Territory of New Mexico, which, in 1855, added the new lands to Dona Ana County. One result is that upon capture, miscreants of all kinds here were sent miles away to Mesilla (south of today's Las Cruces) for prosecution and, if appropriate, incarceration.

Not everyone was entirely satisfied. The downside was that the seat of government was inconvenient, literally hundreds of miles and several days away on horseback. Unfortunately, the western part of the new territory was a lawless land, a refuge for criminals. Everyone from vicious murderers, bank-robbing outlaws, and other undesirable malefactors would run west from Texas and east from California, knowing capture was more difficult in the less-regulated new territory. Leaders in the western half of New Mexico decided it just wouldn't do; they wanted and needed independence, if for no other reason than to establish some kind of effective law.

This raised the question of how to command order. The western portion of New Mexico couldn't secede from the country because they weren't a state. Yet they definitely wanted to separate from New Mexico, to form their own entity. After several politically active, forward-thinking, and ambitious citizens (some of them already serving in territorial government), drew up plans, Congress was first petitioned in 1856 on the matter; Charles Poston, a petitioner who was active in said territorial government (and considered by many to be on the flamboyant side), suggested the name "Arizona."

A belief evolved that the name Arizona is a combination of "arid" and "zone"—because a lot of it, especially the southern part of the state, is in the dry desert. But that's not where the name came from. Actually, it's a corruption of the word "Arizonac," the name of a busy settlement further south in Old Mexico. Arizonac was well known at the time. Perhaps Poston adapted the name to his taste by simply dropping the 'c', thereby also differentiating it from the Mexican city. Perhaps he did so in a burst of whimsy, knowing future generations would misconstrue how the name came about.

Known only as Grandma Muncy, an early settler, shown here in later life, plays with her grandson Howard Wallace. (Courtesy of the Muncy family.)

While all that was going on, railroads were definitely being developed. In the meantime,though, the frontier needed other transport. Edward F. Beale was to play a part in several projects, but his most famous undertaking involved camels.

Beale and Secretary of War Jefferson Davis discussed the need for a sustainable method of travel and whether camels would work. Both men approved the idea enthusiastically. Camels could be purchased in the Near East, then brought to Texas for a period of training and acclimatization. They would be perfect for military travel; tall, rocky mountains and arid desert lands were pure torture for horses and mules, but camels could handle it. It took a while to convince Congress but, in March 1855, an appropriation of $30,000 was finally signed. The first beasts arrived in Texas just over a year after the appropriation, in May 1856, with an additional 44 added the following February.

The camels did do well, work-wise, but the experiment was not a success. A major problem was that the army's horses and mules were skittish around the odd-shaped and distinctly smelly critters. Someone hadn't thought it through. Although horses and mules were okay together, neither got along with the camels at all. Nor did the men assigned to look after them, most of whom had never seen such strange beasts. It was next to impossible to find herdsmen and handlers because only authentic, trained camel drivers could do the job. Another consideration is one that has never been proven. It seems that even though the animals were bred for the desert, their padded feet were inappropriate for the kind of desert found in the western United States. The camels' popularity faded.

Meanwhile, disagreements of a new kind were turning things ugly in the southeastern United States, soon becoming darkly violent. The Civil War was about to explode. When it did, most troops would be recalled. With fewer troops in the west, military transport would be less important. Not only was the camel corps downsized, but numerous presidios, camps, and forts closed. By the end of the Civil War, camels were obsolete. Railroads, belching noise and smoke, had become the new link between East and West. Several camels were sold at auction, and some were merely turned loose in the Arizona desert to run wild.

Since before the war, secession had been a topic bandied about not only in the Deep South but among sympathizers in Arizona. When discussions concerning specific conditions reached an impasse, 11 states seceded to form their own national government. The Union's former secretary of war, Jefferson Davis, was an intelligent and ambitious man. Davis was named president of the new Confederate States of America and his beautiful wife Varina was First Lady.

Farmer Jacob Persinger and wife Iantha, age 22, are shown here shortly after their marriage in 1896. Their daughter Mary would grow up to marry a divorced railroad man with five children. (Courtesy of the Persinger Collection.)

3. Establishment of Camp Huachuca

It is known that around 1860, about the same time war clouds were gathering over the eastern United States, a man named John McLane claimed a parcel of land to homestead in Ramsey Canyon. There would be others, not only in Ramsey Canyon, but Carr Canyon, Miller Canyon, and, eventually, the valley. Believing they'd chosen a new, more peaceful life free of the controversy raging back east, little did they expect to find themselves embroiled in secession while struggling against the warring Native Americans just to stay alive.

At the time, it didn't seem to be important to the homesteaders, but the Territory of New Mexico continued to include all of present-day Arizona. For a number of reasons, it drew the attention of Confederate President Jefferson Davis. Davis wanted the Confederacy to grow laterally, to include not only the original 11 states, but to annex the entire South from coast to coast. He wanted this region not only for its strategic location between Texas and ports in California, but also for its rich gold and silver deposits, the same reason the Spaniards originally desired it. Understanding its value to the South, Davis strongly encouraged an acquisition and, in 1861, Colonel John M. Baylor declared Arizona a Confederate Territory.

That same year, many Federal army officers defected to the Confederacy, including no less than the department commander, Colonel William W. Loring. Others included Colonel George B. Crittenden and Captain Cadmus M. Willcox, both of whom left their names on Arizona's map. Many whose names are less well-known sanctioned the Deep South's cause, and forthwith left the Union army to become "southern gentlemen." It wasn't just the soldiers. The now ghost town Mowry, where tons of rich ore came out of the ground, was named for still another Confederate sympathizer. There was no shortage of them in the Territory, and Davis took full advantage.

On February 14, 1862, President Davis signed a formal government proclamation annexing the Territory. John R. Baylor, no longer a colonel in the army, was named governor. The Confederate flag (called the "Stars and Bars") flew proudly, snapping in the breeze, atop an Arizona flagpole. It would do so for ten days.

Shortly after Davis claimed Arizona for the Confederacy, the westernmost battle of the Civil War took place just north of present-day Tucson. It was Blue against Gray, and the California troops, the all-volunteer Blue, won. Following their victory, President Abraham Lincoln signed a proclamation on February 24, 1862, reclaiming the region for the United States. Lincoln called it the Arizona Territory.

Locally, there remained a strong sympathy for the Confederacy, in part because many "Arizonans" had come from the Deep South. Unfortunately for some of them, July found many troops in southern Arizona abruptly ordered back east. Concerned about a possible Southern takeover and thinking a "scorched earth" policy was better, some forts were destroyed. Fort Breckinridge, with all its supplies, was burned to the ground on July 10. Fort Buchanan was similarly wasted. Scattered settlers who had come west and established family life now felt abandoned. Subject to horrible attacks from the Apaches and added violence from desperadoes, they were perhaps right to do so.

For a long time, the Apaches had watched from their mountain hideouts while making an occasional attack against the invaders. Seeing the turmoil in the east as helpful to ejecting the white man from their territory, some Native Americans felt justified in pursuing their own course of death and destruction. They intensified

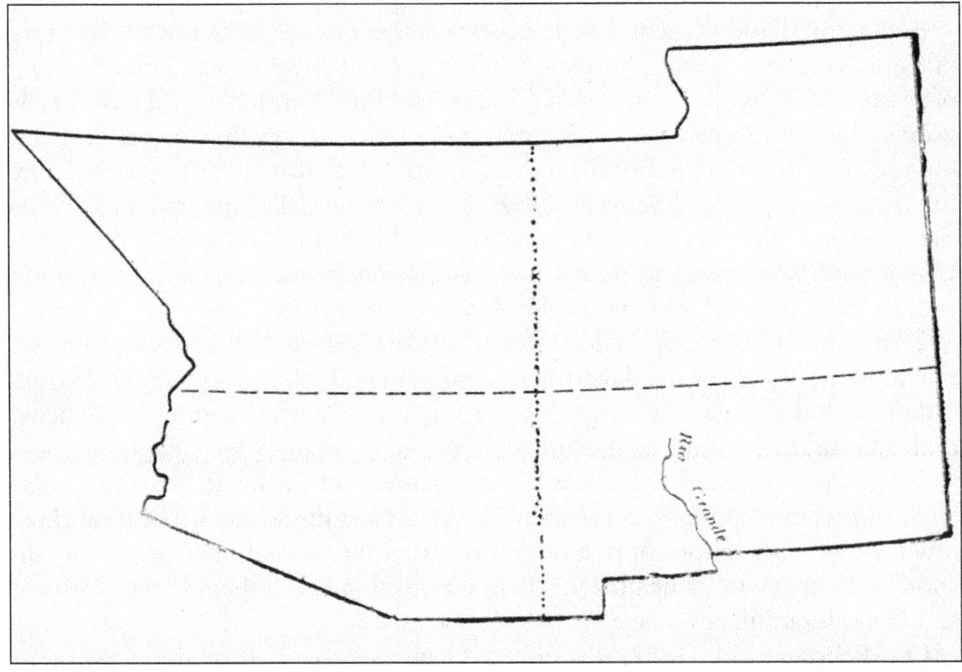

This map of the Territory of New Mexco shows it was part of the Confederacy. When Arizona split off from New Mexico (indicated by the dotted lines), Baylor's Proclamation declared the northern part as the Confederate Territory of New Mexico and the southern part as the Confederate Territory of Arizona. (Drawn by Azevedo.)

their attacks on mines, ranches, villages, lone travelers, and small settlements. All were fodder. All were subject to slaughter and mutilation, to scalping or being barbecued alive. Unfortunately, this action had an unexpected and adverse side effect. Both North and South considered the menacing situation and turned, together, against the Apache Indians.

Colonel Baylor, former soldier and Confederate governor of Arizona Territory, began a particularly ugly form of genocide. His was a treacherous policy of complete extermination, intended to rid the southwestern United States of all Indians. On March 20, 1862, he ordered that all available means of persuasion—including whiskey to rob warriors of their good sense—be used to bring the Indians in for peace talks. Baylor didn't intend to talk peace. His troops were to encircle the camp, guns at the ready; once the Indians were in place, the troops would open fire, slaughtering the adults, men and women, but not the children. He fully intended to take the children alive, selling them as slaves to cover the expense of annihilating their parents. Fortunately, President Davis heard of the plan and summarily stripped Baylor of his command.

Others, not only the Confederates, were of like mind. General James H. Carleton, a Union officer, carried on a modified version of Baylor's program by ordering that all Native American men were to be killed whenever and wherever they were found. No quarter was to be given. It is not known what Carleton intended to do with the women and children, but one can guess that if they survived the battle, they would be enslaved.

In the meantime, boundaries were still being discussed. When on February 24, 1863, Arizona became a territory separate from New Mexico, it allowed Carleton to extend his range of influence into Arizona and he was not loath to do so. Employing "Baylorism," Carleton conceived a plan that would strike a disabling blow to the Apaches. A perfect example of the Indian's claim that white men spoke with a forked tongue, Carleton's men—knowing Mangas Coloradas wanted peace—convinced the nearly 7-foot-tall warrior chief, with his men, to enter a prospector's camp near today's Silver City, New Mexico. Believing he could finally trust that the "White Eyes" wanted to end the bitter conflict, the proud Apache chief didn't anticipate that unbelievable treachery was about to happen. The White Eyes, on the other hand, remembered that Mangas Coloradas was equally vicious to his enemies. One of his favorite tortures, it was said, was to hang a living captive upside down over a fire and watch as the man screamed in agony before finally dying.

Discussions got underway as expected, but they didn't go well, nor were they intended to. Instead, Mangas Coloradas found himself and his men under heavily armed guard, himself the special target of men wielding knives heated in the campfire and used to stab the bound Apache's feet. Drunk on their newfound power, the white guards increased their torture until the chief somehow managed to stand in protest. As a result, they killed him. Forestalling any form of protest by the chief's men, the antagonists immediately unleashed their superior firepower, mowing down the captured and bound Indians.

Cochise was never photographed; however, his son Naiche is shown here. This last chief of free Chiricahua Apaches fought the good fight against overwhelming odds before being conquered and forced onto a reservation.

Still, the White Eyes weren't satisfied. They severed Mangas Coloradas's head (which eventually was placed in the Smithsonian) to create additional havoc among the Indians, who believed the body must be intact for recognition in the great hereafter. Was it all planned? Yes. Obviously so. Though popularly reported as an "attempted escape," it has been described by at least one witness present in the camp when it happened as cold-blooded murder. The facts are that regardless of the perpetrator, regardless of who lured the Indians into camp or who pulled the triggers, and by whatever name the action was called, it was pure Baylorism.

Next, a proud and intelligent man who was both a relative and close friend of Mangas Coloradas would take up the cudgels. This man was Cochise, for whom Cochise County (home of Sierra Vista) is named. Rightfully infuriated at the treacherous assassination of his respected comrade, the brilliant Cochise never again trusted the white man and would wreak bloody havoc on miners, ranchers, the occasional traveler, villages, settlements, and the railroad for the remainder of his days. Now, in addition to suffering vicious raids by Mexican bandits who created devastation before returning to Mexico, settlers would be subjected to an onslaught of incredibly horrific, renewed attacks by the bitterly cunning Apaches.

Often led by Geronimo, the Apaches would come thundering out of the Dragoon Mountains where huge boulders protected them, or the magnificent Chiricahua Mountains. The fearsome warriors would attack and kill White Eyes, scalping their enemies, stealing their livestock (and sometimes their children), and burning everything in sight. Then, following trails known only to them, the Apaches disappeared back into their mountain strongholds. Not adhering to the white man's notion that a border existed, some went not into the mountains, but over them and into Mexico. And like ghosts, some literally went through the mountains because of the numerous caves that snaked through them.

One solution was, of course, reservations. The first one, near the same Gila River that earlier had formed the northern border of Mexico, had already been established by an act of congress. They wouldn't stop there. Several more followed, their boundaries often rather vague and imprecise due to the Wild West's dearth of accurate survey information.

FEBRUARY 20. 1981

PRESENTED WITH GREAT RESPECT TO CIYE NINO COCHISE OF THE TENEH CHOCKONEN APACHE ON HIS 108TH BIRTHDAY. SON OF TAHZA AND GRANDSON OF CHIES-CO-CHISE, GREATEST OF ALL CHIRICAHUA APACHE LEADERS WHO WAS ATTENDED IN HIS LAST DAYS IN 1873 BY A RELATIVE.CAPT. SAMUEL L.ORR. POST SURGEON AT FT. BOWIE AND ACCOMPANIED BY THOMAS J. JEFFORDS.BLOOD BROTHER TO CHIEF COCHISE.

MAY THE GREAT SPIRIT IHIDNAN MARK WELL THE PASSING OF THESE YEARS. AND GRANT MANY MORE TO THE LAST OF THE GREAT CHIRICAHUA APACHE CHIEFS.

This is a copy of a plaque presented on his 108th birthday to Ciye Nino Cochise, grandson of the great Indian chief Chies-co-chise (Cochise) for whom the county where Sierra Vista exists is named.

It often comes as a surprise that perhaps half—maybe more—of today's Cochise County was once a Chiricahua Reservation. The boundaries, as outlined in an Executive Order dated December 4, 1872, were described as:

> Beginning at Dragoon Springs, near Dragoon Pass, and running thence northeasterly along the north base of the Chiricahua Mountains to a point on the summit of the Peloncillo Mountains or Stevens Peak range: then running southeasterly along said range through Stevens Peak to the boundary of New Mexico; thence running westerly along said boundary 55 miles; thence running northerly following substantially the western base of the Dragoon Mountains, to the place of beginning.

Keeping the free-ranging warriors, the hunter-gatherer Apache, on a reservation with borders was another story entirely. One problem was that the White Eyes were wrong in their conception that "Apache" was a collective term with loyalty holding them to an "all for one and one for all" lifestyle. They did not understand

Explorers in the Dragoon Mountains encountered a strange landscape consisting mostly of boulders weighing many tons each. The boulders, seemingly left after being pushed together during the Ice Age, would prove impassible for wheeled conveyances.

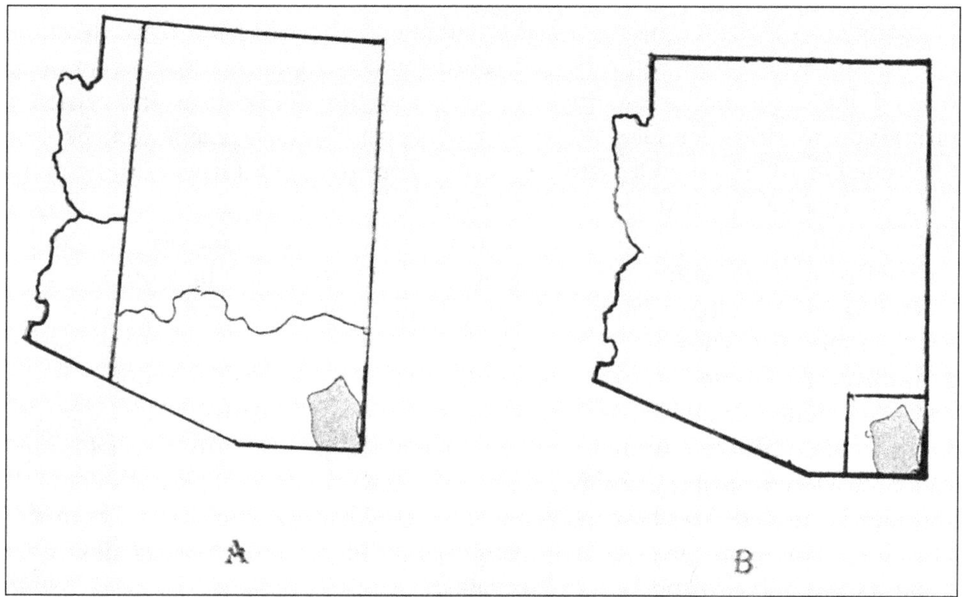

Map A shows the original four counties of the Territory of Arizona, which were Yavapai (the largest, followed by Pima County just below it. The upper left is Mohave County, and below it is Yuma County. The shaded section is the Chiricahua Apache reservation. Map B shows the size of the Chiricahua Apache's reservation as compared to today's Cochise County. (Drawn by Azevedo.)

that there were subdivisions within the overall grouping, more like family members who marry and move on to create their own subdivision. Nor did the White Eyes understand that each of these family sub-groups was very nearly autonomous; one might join another in battle, but the groups were just as likely to fight against one another. (An interesting fact is that when an Apache man married, he not only joined, but actually became a part of the wife's family, as opposed to the patriarchal society the Europeans were used to. The married Apache was expected to join his wife's family in whatever causes or battles they were addressing.)

Apache raids, often under the leadership of Geronimo, continued in defense of their homelands. However, not all abided with his decisions; some chose life on the reservation as a way of protecting their loved ones' lives. Following Cochise's death from probable natural causes on June 8, 1874, the reservation in southeastern Arizona was summarily deactivated, dismantled, and abolished. The roundup, not of cattle but of humans, continued. When the honored chief was no longer available to negotiate, a group of 325 Chiricahua Apache were sent off in June 1876 to other reservations. This policy proved dangerous however, as the government did not realize that some of these Apache groups were hostile toward one another. Trouble followed; indeed, it seemed to increase.

Clearly, something needed to be done. Ranches, mines, and villages were all in dire need of protection. General George Crook had been in command of the

Department of Arizona; he'd worked to subdue the Apaches and place them on reservations where they could be controlled (and, as some say, "taken care of"). In so doing, he gained substantial respect among the White Eyes and earned a promotion to Brigadier General. As often happens with a promotion, he was reassigned in 1875 to the Department of the Platte and would have nothing to do with Arizona for the next seven years. The best soldiers had also been deployed to the north. Obviously, someone was needed who would take on a politically charged assignment with tactical and strategic disadvantages. Who would it be?

The army's leader, Colonel August Kautz, was stationed in territorial headquarters at Prescott where he did ongoing political battle with the governor and others. He needed someone he could trust. Poring over voluminous notes and maps, Kautz decided that conditions in the sparsely settled territory to the south would probably require no more than two troops of cavalry. Several camps had been closed during the Civil War but a new one, more centrally located, was clearly needed. Yes, he considered, they could form a new garrison in the Huachuca Mountains, from which the troops could fan out to protect all settlers in both the San Pedro and Santa Cruz valleys.

After considering several names, Kautz chose a young but experienced captain from Fort Lowell (near Tucson) named Captain Samuel M. Whitside to command the expedition. The chosen man was actually Canadian, having been born (on January 9, 1839) in Toronto, Ontario. After rising through the ranks, he had married Carrie McGavock (from Nashville, Tennessee) on November 24, 1868, in San Antonio, Texas. He was reassigned to Fort Lowell on January 15, 1876. On February 12, 1877, Kautz signed the order sending Whitside, his men, and a second group from Camp Grant to an area in the general vicinity of old Fort Crittenden. Perhaps they could make use of Camp Wallen, an earlier facility the army had abandoned after an epidemic outbreak of malaria.

Traveling in a general southeasterly direction from Fort Lowell, the mounted troops wended their way through the Whetstone Mountains. Whitside, sending regular dispatches back to headquarters, reported no resistance at all, nothing to change their course or their mission. Indeed, he claimed, no Indians had been sighted along the way (but he failed to explain that they had followed established trails). Arriving at what had been Camp Wallen, they found no sign of habitability. There were crumbing walls, broken shards of glass, a dented pot—as if the former residents had left in a hurry. Still, Whitside and his men looked the place over; it didn't take long.

Investigating the rubble, the soldiers quickly discarded any idea of establishing a new post on what had become little more than a trash dump. Indeed, Whitside, after careful evaluation, was of like mind. However, deciding against heading west and closer to the Santa Cruz, he chose to lead his troops further south, toward the distant mountains he saw tickling the sky. There, his gut feeling told him, they would find the perfect location.

So, following Whitside's hunch, they headed out. About 8 miles further south, on a gloriously warm day with wildflowers scenting the air and birds warbling their mating calls, the captain found himself at the mouth of Huachuca Canyon. He was right; it was an absolutely perfect spot to establish a new camp!

At the back would be the formidably tall Huachuca Mountains, forming protective cover from raiding parties of whatever kind, and in the front, a wide, sweeping vista where a guard's eyes could easily see the smoke from campfires or the dust clouds of approaching riders long before they got close enough to do serious damage. Here, there was not only an abundance of tall, nourishing grass for the horses, but a generous mountain stream to provide all the cold, fresh water needed for both man and beast. There were veritable forests of mature trees, perfect for the lumber needed to build a permanent camp.

And so, on Saturday, March 3, 1877, Captain Whitside ordered his men to halt, dismount, and make camp. They did. That night, the captain wrote in his logbook: "Camp Huachuca, Huachuca Mountains, Arizona Territory, Capt. S.M. Whitside, Commanding Officer." It was officially an army installation

As soon as possible, he sent for his wife. She joined him on the rugged frontier post, becoming the first woman to live there. Accustomed as she was to the beautiful Tennessee countryside, this doctor's daughter had chosen to be the wife of a soldier, and she adapted well. Other wives and families soon followed her lead.

In the meantime, the first few months found both men and their families living temporarily in tents. In fact, the first child born at Camp Huachuca made her

More permanent barracks replaced tents; these were built from lumber harvested from the trees in the Huachuca Mountains. It was during sawmill operations that Captain Whitside was injured. This photo dates to 1880. (Courtesy of the Fort Huachuca Historical Museum.)

These original Fort Huachuca buildings (barracks) still stand today, but are used as offices. (Courtesy of Ron Price.)

initial appearance in a tent; named Helen May Craig, she was the daughter of a lieutenant and his wife.

While making do with tent life, several men were assigned construction duty. Part of this consisted of making adobe bricks from mud and straw, then baking them in the hot sun. Soon, they had enough to build living quarters, barracks, and other things necessary to a permanent establishment.

Unfortunately, the rainy (that is, monsoon) season in the Huachucas began—as it still does—early in July and went through mid-September. In addition to the jagged lightning and crashing thunder, there was rain every day. Relentlessly, the water pounded down, roofs soaking up all they could before collapsing. Storerooms flooded, ruining everything inside. Stables fell down, killing some of the horses. And the little house into which Lieutenant Craig, his wife, and daughter had happily moved was gone. They were back to living in a tent.

Adding to their misery were myriad "critters." Bugs and snakes, some quite deadly, come out during the summer monsoons. It certainly wasn't the kind of genteel, civilized life experienced back east. On the frontier, there was no reason to wear a ball gown. However, the women adapted as the wives of soldiers always do. They helped each other, commiserated with each other, celebrated with each other, and cried with each other.

One of the first things established at the new facility was the Post Cemetery. The first burial was that of Private Thomas Kelly on December 22, 1877. Three years later, on December 28, Colonel Whitside and his wife Carrie laid to rest their tiny son Dallas. Other graves are unnamed, some of them of Mexican children moved there when their own final resting place was damaged or destroyed. A few identities have never been established, but the U.S. Army gave them a proper burial and has, for more than 100 years, honored them with a marker and maintenance of the gravesite. The headstone simply notes "An Unknown Mexican Child."

During this time, a sawmill was created. The soldiers felled huge pine trees growing on the mountainsides to be used in construction of more substantial buildings. Whitside was a working officer, but his labors were temporarily suspended when he broke his leg and was taken to Fort Lowell to recuperate. Coming back to Camp Huachuca in February, he assumed rugged frontier duties before his bones had completely healed, and he suffered a serious relapse. This time, the army took no chances. Whitside was sent to Los Angeles to recuperate, and he wasn't allowed to return to Camp Huachuca till early July (just in time for the monsoons).

Perhaps Whitside's injury, recuperation, relapse, and second recuperation gave impetus to building the camp's first permanent construction. It was a hospital that cost $1,288.77 to build. It still exists, renamed the Carleton House (ironically after the Carleton who ordered the assasination of Mangas Coloradas).

A row of double barracks were built in 1883. In the six years between the time Camp Huachuca was established and the barracks' construction, quarters for enlisted personnel were utterly miserable. Winter in the mountains can be cold; whether or not there was snow and ice at the camp's level, there was snow and ice on top of the mountain. A piercingly strong wind whistled down off the mountaintop, exacerbating the bone-chilling temperature. It easily came through the seams of the canvas-and-adobe buildings thrown up as shelter. In the summer, the problem was a complete reverse: dust chokingly swirled its way through the tiniest crack. Then in early July, humidity would be added. Poisonous creatures were constant roommates, so the soldiers found themselves shaking everything before dressing in the morning or before going to bed at night.

When new accommodations were built, they were in high contrast; the men actually had heat in winter and ventilation in summer. They enjoyed lots of space while non-commissioned officers even maintained some privacy, as befitted their rank. The new barracks were built sturdily, with stone masonry foundations, wood frame walls, and beaverboard lining the insides. There were open porches called verandas on both floors, upper and lower, to provide additional protection from the summer sun and the monsoons.

These buildings still stand. They are used today for administrative purposes and the insides have been remodeled from time to time, but the general exterior of the buildings has not changed from the date of construction in 1883. Today, the buildings are part of Historical Fort Huachuca and are irreplaceable; however, at the time of construction the most expensive cost just over $13,000 to build.

Arizona was growing. When originally named an official territory, it had but four counties, but by 1880 these had been subdivided into seven. Pima County ran from the New Mexico border nearly across southern Arizona, ending at the Yuma County line. It took in what is now Cochise County and Santa Cruz

County. It was difficult to live there because it was a very long ride from, for instance, Willcox to Tucson when there was a court case. Especially since not only the principals in the case but the officials, witnesses, etc.—no matter their age or health condition—had to make the round trip. After petitioning the government, the territorial residents eventually were heard; subsequently, the counties were divided again. This southeast corner of Arizona became Cochise County, named after the late Chiricahua chief. Cochise County's western border ended at Pima County's eastern border. There was no Santa Cruz County yet. It was established that Tombstone would be the county seat. Not an impossible number of miles away, Fort Huachuca stayed in place since territorial borders had no effect on military installations, fixed just inside the western edge of Cochise County.

In the early to mid-1880s, Fort Huachuca kept its mission to protect settlers. The Native Americans were still at war, with Apaches attacking and killing some men as close as Canelo, just outside what is now Fort Huachuca's West Gate. The year 1886 brought changes. Geronimo, a leader but never a chief, had continued bloody raids against the invading white man. In March of 1886 he surrendered, only to escape with some of his warriors. The rampage began again, continuing

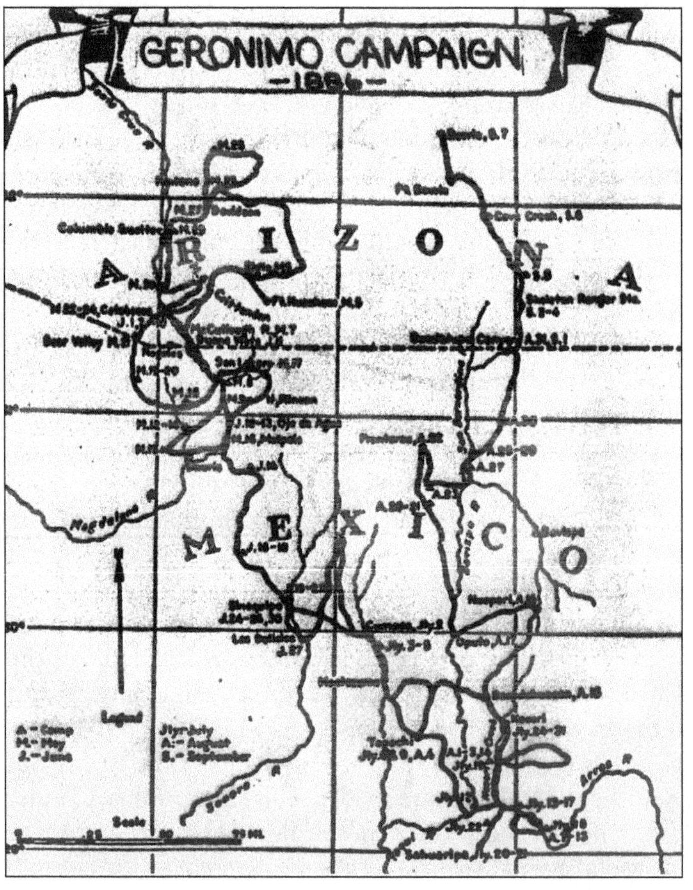

This map shows how the Geronimo Campaign, part of the Apache Wars, crossed international boundaries in 1886, taking place both in Mexico and the Arizona Territory. (Courtesy of the Fort Huachuca Historical Museum.)

Lieutenant Charles B. Gatewood was a major player in the surrender of Geronimo. A street on Fort Huachuca is named for him. (Courtesy of the Fort Huachuca Historical Mueum.)

all summer. In May, Geronimo and his band slaughtered some miners near Bisbee. In June, they appeared near the railroad tracks a few miles east of Willcox. On horseback, heading south, they shot at the railroad trackwalker but did not hit him; the man was able to flag down the next eastbound train and report the incident to the conductor.

Over a period of two years (1888–1889), the Copper Queen Consolidated Mining Company, a subsidiary of Phelps Dodge Corporation, built the Arizona & Southwestern Railroad. The Arizona & New Mexico Railroad already existed, but the nearest loading point was to the north in Fairbank, Arizona, which is now a ghost town. The new 36-mile-long line would connect the copper mines in Bisbee to the loading point in Fairbank. To further facilitate the transport of anodes from the smelters, they later constructed another 19 miles of track into Benson, Arizona to connect with the Southern Pacific Railroad. On June 25,

1901, Phelps Dodge signed over the properties of the Arizona & Southwestern Railroad to the newly-founded El Paso & Southwestern Railroad.

Perhaps not strangely, the Native Americans usually steered clear of the steam trains that rumbled through southern Arizona. To them, the trains were invincible, roaring juggernauts that breathed smoke and didn't bleed when struck with bullets and arrows. Attacking them was futile, so they respectfully let the trains go about their business.

The summer of 1901 was a definite turning point. Still fighting long past the time the war should have ended, even Geronimo and his followers were getting tired. His wife and children had been killed, his best friends were dead, the White Eyes were winning. No longer able to fight the good fight, Geronimo surrendered one last time and his ragtag band was escorted by army troops to Fort Bowie. In September 1886, they boarded one of those loud steam trains on their way to Florida. The natives sold most of their belongings to various people at stations along the way.

Geronimo never returned to his beloved homeland, and the Apache Wars were nearly over.

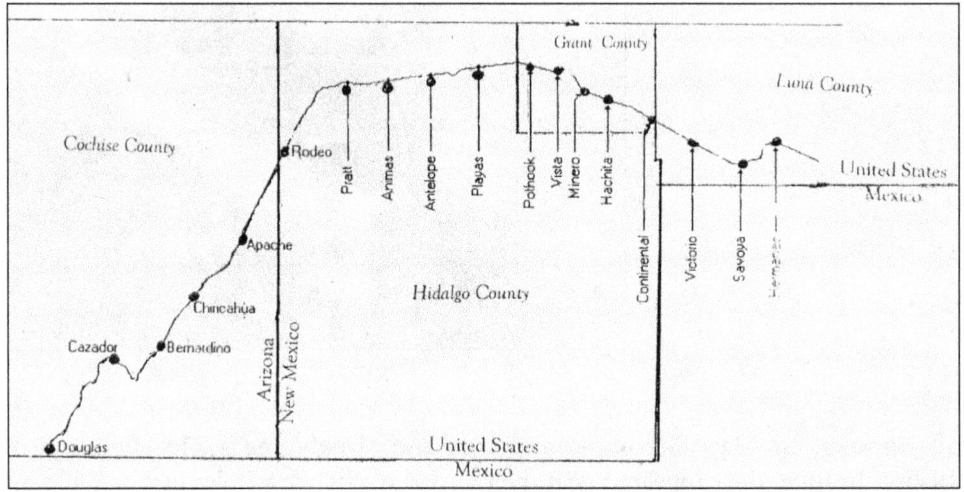

This map shows the route of the El Paso & Southwestern Railroad as it roared west through the upper boot heel of New Mexico with its last stop before crossing into Arizona at the tiny town of Rodeo. Its next stop was in an equally small community named Apache, Arizona. (Drawn by Azevedo.)

4. Earthquake of 1887

The occasional raid still occurred, but now immigrants poured in. Overnight, towns would spring up, the ore would be mined, and (quite often) the towns were deserted to become ghost towns. On the other hand, a few—Tombstone, Benson, Bisbee, St. David, Charleston—thrived, and life was good. Life was exciting.

In 1887, the month of March certainly was going according to the usual plan. Days were already warm in southern Arizona, with just enough nip in the air at night to make sleeping wonderful. There may have been a slight dusting of snow on the mountain's upper levels, in the crags and shadows, but not here. Here, at an altitude of more than 5,000 feet, trees were already turning green, wildflowers bloomed, and there was plenty of cold, fresh water splashing in the stream. Food was plentiful, with game such as deer, squirrels, javelinas, perhaps a bear, and more easy to come by, supplementing harsh winter diets. Though dealing or preparing to deal with the area's assorted problems, life at Fort Huachuca actually held some very pleasant moments. April was more of the same.

Certainly, on May 3, 1887, the day began routinely at daybreak. Expecting nothing extraordinary, the men at Camp Huachuca tended their horses as usual, seeing they were fed, perhaps talking to them, probably joking and grousing amongst themselves. Once the animals were taken care of, the men returned to the mess where breakfast awaited, a meal that could have involved biscuits or flapjacks but was just as likely to consist of hardtack, some kind of meat, and pots of thick, black coffee, boiled with eggshells and drunk from dented tin cups. Maybe, just maybe, there were some beans left from supper the night before.

It was shortly after payday and, if the paymaster had delivered, several of the troops would have departed immediately for Tombstone or other rowdy locations. If they had already returned, a few probably groaned, doctoring a skull-pounding headache with "the hair of the dog." The morning routine did not take long. Within minutes, the soldiers began saddling up, preparing to carry out their orders for the day. Perhaps one commented to another that the air felt different but—pshaw! It was probably his imagination.

Yet it wasn't long until residents of scattered ranches and settlements began noticing an increased agitation among their livestock. Even chickens—never the most intelligent of creatures—were affected, clucking frantically and running about. Dogs were nervous, hiding under a porch when one was available. Horses pranced restlessly, tossed their heads, rolled their eyes, and snorted their unrest.

Shortly, the earth began a mild quiver, hardly noticed, that quickly increased in intensity until it seemed the whole world was about to fall apart. Giant cracks appeared in the earth, sometimes with water spewing from the opening; buildings crumbled and fell; and near Benson, a sidelined train actually rocked back and forth on the tracks. Hundreds of feet deep in the earth, in the man-made tunnels of the rich Tombstone-area silver mines, loosened rocks fell from the walls while men scrambled frantically to reach the surface.

In Palominas, rancher Henry Pyeatt, who had married less than a month earlier, was passing the day (and a number of tall tales) with some friends. It was pleasant there on the front porch of the general store. Sitting on a pile of lumber, Pyeatt was startled by what he first thought was thunder. Looking around, he and his friends saw no clouds, just clear sky. Seconds later, the ground was moving, almost like waves in the ocean. The adobe store building where they sat suffered its first damage when a big chunk fell off, nearly hitting the men. The young and brave men were now scared men running to and fro, unsure what to do. They wanted to run away, but where could one run to? It seemed as if the whole world was being shaken! It was the longest 14 seconds (timed by a resident with a good watch) in history.

Certain factions, perhaps more superstitious or impressionable than others, would come to say it was retribution for the white man's invasion, for his taking what did not belong to him. Well, whatever its scientific cause, the great earthquake did occur exactly two months after the tenth anniversary of the date Captain Whitside first established Camp Huachuca, and there has not been another, in this area, since.

Regardless, when the quake was over and the dust settled, assessments were duly taken. Officials discovered that mining towns, which had fixed structures above ground and tunnels dug underneath, suffered incredible damage, yet no one was killed. In fact, it is said that later the same day, Tombstone gambling halls left standing were doing a bang-up business.

One that didn't make it was Charleston, a town built on the banks of the San Pedro River between Tombstone and today's Sierra Vista. There, a mere 30 seconds of violent shaking laid serious damage to every building in town. In what had a few minutes earlier been a thriving, bustling community, not a single home or place of business was left unscathed. The formerly prosperous and lively mining town was reduced to little more than ruins.

Adding to Charlestonians' misfortune, the quake loosened humongous boulders that came crashing down the mountainsides. Rock against rock they tumbled, bouncing off each other, striking incredible sparks along the way. Sparks landed in dry grass, a danger in early May because the summer monsoons had not yet arrived. Soon, small wisps of smoke floated upward, followed by little tongues of flame that caused some to fear volcanoes had erupted and they would be covered in molten lava. There were no volcanoes, but the flames quickly grew into a wall of fire. Still in shock, citizens watched helplessly as the blaze destroyed everything in its path. Charleston did not recover. Its residents chose not to rebuild. Instead, they abandoned the site and relocated to nearby towns that had fared better.

More was to come. The entire area lies above a huge underground aquifer that often plagued miners, flooding their tunnels, sometimes drowning workers. During the powerful quake, the earth's crust literally cracked. Unleashed, the aquifer burst from its confines, in some places spraying water high into the air and creating new streams. At the same time, established rivers and creeks simply quit flowing or realigned themselves to follow new pathways.

Not everything attributed to the earthquake was bad; some saw the whole event as a boon, an answer to fervent prayers. For instance, in the small village of St. David, people were suffering and dying. Actually, the little town was built on marshland. All the ponds in yards and fields provided plenty of water for personal use and growing crops but, at the same time, were a rich breeding ground for disease-carrying mosquitoes. Malaria soon felled many a citizen. One devout Mormon leader named David Snow prayed fervently that his town and his people be relieved from the pestilence and suffering. With the earthquake, Apostle Snow got what he asked for.

This photo, dated 1890, shows the inside of typical quarters where the families of officers lived at Camp Huachuca. (Courtesy of the Fort Huachuca Historical Museum.)

True, homes and other buildings fell as they had in Charleston. The St. David school was destroyed. Irrigation canals were badly damaged, water having been flung out of them. However, no one was seriously injured and, that night, the faithful could sleep under an unclouded sky filled with twinkling stars.

Surveying the extensive damage next day, St. David residents discovered that not only had water levels increased, but wonderfully clear and fresh new artesian ponds had miraculously appeared. The brackish ponds of yesterday, often covered in green slime, were gone. Men, women, and children now scratched at fewer mosquito bites, and when new malaria cases occurred, they soon disappeared.

Some claim David Snow was a prophet, that he predicted the earthquake; certainly, he often preached that the raging pestilence and devastating sickness would end dramatically, though he knew not how. When the earthquake was over, Apostle Snow found himself the object of respectful awe. He set about proclaiming to all who would listen that God used the earthquake to fulfill his, Snow's, personal prophecy. Indeed, he was satisfied that events happened just as he had predicted. Any other explanation was inconceivable. Perhaps Snow was right.

This grave marker for an "Unknown Mexican Child," who was relocated to these premises when storms or other disasters destroyed the original grave, is maintained by the U.S. Army in the same manner as its most honored soldiers. (Courtesy of Ron Price.)

5. Oliver Fry and Family Arrive

Henry Pyeatt, who had been at the Palominas store when the earthquake hit, worked at a couple of other ranches during the next dozen years. Then, in 1899, he and his wife Mary bought a ranch outside the West Gate of Fort Huachuca near a little community called Canelo (Spanish for cinnamon, so named because settlers thought the hills were the color of cinnamon). Pyeatt would add to his ranch over the years, ending with nearly 9,000 acres. All the area children attended classes in the little one-room school at Canelo (the building still stands, and hosts a periodic gathering of "pioneer" families). On the Pyeatt ranch is a cave that, years later, would acquire quite a reputation.

A few years after the Pyeatts established themselves at Canelo, west of the Fort, a family named Carmichael put down roots at the eastern perimeter of the military reservation. It was 1910 when Bill and Margaret Carmichael filed on their land and the area was called Overton (another name before it became Sierra Vista). The Carmichaels bought some property, including a general store and post office, from a man named Riley and then added additional ranchlands. Bill had been in the army, stationed at Fort Huachuca; they liked it here and when he was mustered out, he contracted to bring the army payroll from El Paso to Fort Huachuca each month via mule train. Margaret would go on to earn the title "First Lady" of the community.

However, it was just past the turn of the century and the wild west had already settled down a tad. The Apache Wars were over with maybe a single, and very occasional, fracas here and there. Telegraph wires connected people in this remote corner of Arizona to the outside world. Tombstone, once a hell-raising, silver-mining boomtown, had declined so much that it had fewer than 1,000 residents; in the process, it toned down and became quite mellow (comparatively speaking). Bisbee, on the other hand, found itself on the upswing. Riding a growing demand for copper used in telegraph and telephone wires, Bisbee was growing quite prosperous. Copper wasn't the only mineral to figure in the development of the local community, although it was the longest lasting. Gold did its share, but not for a few years.

Laura Persinger Bates was cousin to Mary Persinger. Although this photo is undated, it was most likely taken around 1910. (Courtesy of the Persinger Collection.)

Regardless, there were people moving into the area, though usually onto properties that left them rather sparsely settled by today's standards. Still, the U.S. government and others encouraged more and more people to move west, to homestead a section, a half-section, or even a quarter-section. The catchphrase of the day was "Go west, young man; go west." Several had already done so. One was Frank Moson, whose widowed (or some say divorced) mother had remarried when Frank was still a youth. Another was Pete Johnson, whose ranch ran from Naco (a tiny village partly in Arizona, partly in Sonora) to the San Pedro River. Other ranch owners were named Williams and Fike and Martin and Leiendecker. Names were constantly being added to the roster, and it wasn't just the ranch owners but also the families who lived and worked on the spreads. On many of these, more so the closer they were to the border, herds of wild cattle roamed back and forth. Ranches weren't yet fenced and unbranded cattle don't understand lines of demarcation. At roundup time, the U.S. cowboys simply gathered what was currently on their side, and drove the herds to the nearest railhead in Willcox.

The young Frank Moson, who became a large landowner as an adult, gave his name to Moson Road. His land holdings included the Y-Lightning Ranch. (Courtesy of Mary Estes.)

Silver mining may have lost its former luster, but there was growing interest and unlimited possibilities in cattle ranching. And there were communities here and there, small ones, some with reputations already established, others practically unknown anywhere else. Hundreds of miles north, families read about the warm weather, wide open spaces, and abundance of opportunities. One such family would have a great impact on what is now Sierra Vista.

The fact is, Iowa can be a forbiddingly cold and bitter place to live; January brings swirling snow and thick ice to the wind-swept plains. It was a veritable plague to anyone having to be out in the elements, and a coal-mining town is never the most uplifting or inviting. In the bitter winter of 1901, an intense storm left snowdrifts up to 6 feet deep and horses, straining to pull wagons over frozen ground, slipped on the ice in the wagon ruts. The wind whistled eerily around corners and through cracks.

In this dismal atmosphere, a family of six people—mother, father, and four children—read about warmer climes and decided to follow the government's urging to "go west." Once the decision was made, they did not hesitate in preparing for the journey and soon found themselves standing excitedly at the train station. Bundled in warm coats and scarves to protect against the chill, not minding the stormy gray skies, there were apples in the kids' cheeks, excitement in the air. Laughing, jumping up and down, the younger members of the family vied to be first in hearing the train's whistle because that meant the iron horse would be chugging around the bend. Then there it was! Brakes screeched, the train pulled in, stopped, and was shortly ready to take on passengers. Chattering loudly, their breath fogging the cold winter air, the Fry family eagerly climbed aboard the iron horse.

Within minutes, two toots of the train's whistle found Oliver and Elizabeth Fry ensconced in comfortable seats while their children (Tom, Cora, Erwin, and Edna) rubbed frost from the windows to watch as they left the station. They were heading more south than west, but no matter. It would be warmer and Oliver could grow his own crops in Texas, not far from where his brother lived west of Houston. It was a definite change for them. From coal mining in Iowa, they became farmers in Barker, Texas, learning how on the job. They grew crops, raised farm animals, and, five months of each year, the children attended school. When not in school, the children had their own chores to do at home. It was hard work, but for the 12 years they stayed in Barker, they appear to have thrived. Indeed, the family grew as five more children were added, making a total of nine.

In 1909, while the Fry family was still in Texas, a group never specifically identified but simply called "influential persons" allegedly made a strong attempt at having Fort Huachuca moved. As reported in the *Tombstone Epitaph*, they wanted it moved lock, stock, and barrel from the mouth of the Huachuca Canyon to a site east of Bisbee—actually, halfway between Bisbee and Douglas.

Calling the relocation a "plum" and apparently without any information whatsoever about the availability of gold, the excited reporter posited that the fort's current site was ideal for a gold-mining camp. He seemed to believe the move was inevitable (actually saying "That the fort will be moved there is no doubt. . . .") and suggesting several reasons why it would be perfect for everyone concerned. One reason was that Fort Huachuca would be nearer a railroad; another reason, according to that reporter, was ". . . the air is warmer in the vicinity of Bisbee and Douglas than in the lofty Huachucas."

Perhaps he could be excused for the latter observation but only if he was new to the territory and unfamiliar with the year-round changes in southeast Arizona. Anyone who'd been here for at least one complete year would know that at the lower altitude between Bisbee and Douglas, the late spring and summer temperatures are more than "warmer." They often reach 100 degrees and more, hot enough it can literally hurt to breathe and making the cool temperatures of the mountains much more desirable.

Maybe it was just a slow day for news when the reporter wrote that article. Maybe he received a tip without checking its authenticity. Regardless, the never-identified "influential persons" didn't have as much clout as he supposed and nothing ever came of it. He was right about one thing though; the groundwork was already being laid and momentous events were (comparatively speaking) not far off. In the meantime, Fort Huachuca stayed where it had always been and would have a tremendous impact on the future growth of what is now Sierra Vista.

Barely three years later, at 10:00 a.m. on February 14 in 1912, history was made. In a long anticipated move, at that appointed hour President William H. Taft signed the Arizona Statehood Bill. A half-century of struggle was over. A sweep of the pen had just made Arizona the forty-eighth state, with George W.P. Hunt as its first governor. (Actually, history tells us he was elected a full two months prior, in preparation for just this event, and he would be re-elected six more times).

Arizona certainly celebrated! Mines and factories shut down, letting their people off work. Schools were dismissed. Parades, fireworks, picnics, and other events were the order of the day.

Word spread like wildfire. Back in Barker, Texas, Oliver Fry and his good friend, Everett Easton, listened. In Arizona, they heard, one could homestead a parcel of land easily. All one had to do was choose one, file a claim on it, and "prove up" on it. (One could not simply file on property and neither live on it nor do nothing with it. One had to "prove" one's intentions to homestead.) Why, one could get rich raising beef cattle. Fry and Easton decided to investigate. History doesn't explain why they chose their destination, but, in June of that same year, the two men bought rail tickets. They traveled by train to a station—actually, a mere "siding"—they had learned about. Called Huachuca, it was on the south

This artist's rendering shows the former Huachuca Siding, near the banks of the Babocomari on the west side of today's Highway 90 north of Sierra Vista, about where the Hideout is now found. (Drawing courtesy of Ricardo Alonzo.)

bank of the Babocomari River (the exact spot is north of today's Huachuca City, about where the current Hideout Bar & Grill is found).

Disembarking, the two men stretched to unkink tired muscles and looked around. It was a beautiful valley. However, it wasn't just exactly what they wanted. They wouldn't settle on the Babocomari. Fry and Easton wanted to go further, to discover greener pastures. After all, several others were already settled here. But they would need a method of transport. Asking around, they found one of the families living near the riverbank who agreed to rent them a horse and buggy. Off they went, heading generally south, skirting the edges of Fort Huachuca to find a perfect tract of land to homestead.

Finding themselves at the main gate of Fort Huachuca, the military reservation separated from the outside only by barbed wire, the men hesitated. There wasn't much to see. A dirt road led from the main gate, going east in the direction of the San Pedro river, which they had crossed on the train. Indeed, another railroad station was out there; Lewis Springs lay between the army post and the river. Maybe, the men decided, they would go see what was down that road.

They found exactly what they were looking for. Quickly laying claim to their 160 acres, they drove in marking stakes. Oliver Fry chose his land on the north side of the dirt road (now Fry Boulevard, the "main drag" of Sierra Vista), and his best friend claimed acreage just across the road on the south side. Hurrying

The original Carmichael Store is shown here in Garden Canyon (pre-Sierra Vista). The sign over the door says "Post Office" and because of its location, gave the community its name. It housed the main store, a butchershop, two small sitting rooms, a kitchen, a dining room, and a warehouse. A bedroom was built on after the original construction. The Frys would eventually lease this facility from the Carmichaels before building their own store and post office. This building is one of very few historical buildings still standing and currently houses the Daisy Mae Steakhouse. (Courtesy of the Henry Hauser Museum.)

All the grown steers and older cows were driven to the cattle yard next to the railroad at the Siding (Huachuca City) where a buyer waited with empty cattle cars. (Courtesy Henry Hauser Museum.)

to Tombstone (then the county seat), they filed papers before going back to Huachuca Siding and returning the horse and buggy to their owners.

Back in Barker, Texas, they took a few months to settle things, including sale of the farm. Oliver bought a herd of two dozen Jersey cows, thinking he might form a dairy to sell milk to the army post. Unfortunately, cattle were on the quarantine list; he found he wouldn't be able to bring them across the Arizona state line. Forced to sell his beautiful Jerseys, he immediately busied himself investigating myriad possibilities before switching to another plan. Yet one thing didn't change; Oliver Fry had filed for his homestead allotment and he and his family would relocate to southern Arizona.

Late that fall, Oliver and two of his sons were ready. Hiring several rail cars, they took tools, livestock and feed, farm equipment, and whatever they needed to carry them over until they were established. The two boys, Tom and Erwin, rode in the freight car where they could stretch out on bales of hay, Oliver in a passenger car where he slept sitting up. The trip took six days. Arriving at Huachuca Siding after dark on November 18, 1912, the exhausted trio off-loaded everything they owned before going to sleep under the wagons. It was after midnight. The next morning, they rose at daylight to hitch up the wagons and headed south to their new home.

Once there, Oliver set about erecting a shelter for his family. Lumber for the two room structure, home for a family of 11, came from a sawmill in Garden Canyon. At the time, there was no water on his plot of land, not a creek nor a well, but Oliver bought water from Ray Shadley, a man who had earlier built a shack

In this photo, dated 1916, troops are getting ready to leave Fort Huachuca for Mexico to take part in what was gently called the "Border Conflict." (Courtesy of the Fort Huachuca Historical Museum.)

for his family in an arroyo about midway between the Main Gate and East Gate. After the shack was built, Shadley turned his attention to digging and hit water less than 50 feet down. Though he never homesteaded the land, Shadley had his own well and could haul water in wooden barrels to others who had no well.

Other businesses sprang up near Fort Huachuca. According to one source, there was at the time a shabby row of wooden shacks built along North Garden Avenue, adjacent to each other and sharing the same roof. They were painted white. From these, the settlement got its first name: White City. Never an official name, it was a colloquialism established through common usage by the nearby military. Others report that this situation existed, but not until World War II. In whatever time frame, the district did exist. It existed by that name and for that purpose, giving color to the city. The ironic truth is that White City was the local red light district; the shacks were houses of ill repute, where "ladies of the night" practiced their shady professions. Diseases were spread, unwanted pregnancies terminated, and the "ladies" would, later on, come to make use of Fry Cemetery (which still tenuously exists). The houses would be destroyed.

Upon his arrival, Oliver Fry diligently applied himself and, by January 1913, the Fry homestead was ready. Fry sent word back to Texas. Elizabeth, seven of their children who had remained behind, and Everett Easton and his family all packed up their belongings, boarded the train, and said goodbye to Barker, Texas. They were heading west. This time, they didn't go directly to Huachuca Siding; they disembarked at Lewis Springs, on the east side of the San Pedro, where the Frys' eldest son, Tom, was waiting with a horse and wagon. It was winter and Oliver, wanting his family's arrival to be pleasantly warm, stayed at home to tend the fireplace. The Fry home was located just about where the Family Dollar Store is today.

Later that same year (1913), a railroad spur was built from the station at Lewis Springs through what is now Sierra Vista (its tracks are still there) and on to Fort Huachuca. In large part, soldiers still rode horses, but rail travel would allow them to deploy more quickly. Therefore, while the line might not have been extended were it not for the army, once built, it could bring in supplies from as far away as Benson or Tombstone or even Willcox. Or further.

An entrepreneur at heart, Oliver Fry was quick to understand that the new railroad spur meant new business possibilities. It wasn't long till he partitioned off part of the boys' bedroom to establish an early version of a convenience store. He could sell, among other things, produce from the family garden (once it was planted and harvested), milk from their cows (the family dairymaid was daughter Edna), homemade mincemeat that Elizabeth prepared in the kitchen, and probably a particular liquid that Oliver cooked up in a shack in the back yard.

More and more homesteaders found their way west, ready for the adventure and eager to establish claims. For instance, within a year after the Frys put down roots, two men, Oscar Tomberlin and Ed Higgins, came out of California to stake their quarter section claims further east on that bumpy dirt road leading from Fort Huachuca to Lewis Springs. Like others before them, the friends chose land side-by-side. Their land lies where Hastings Books & Music, Ace Hardware, and Pier 1 Imports are today, in the southwest quadrant formed by the intersections of the Highway 90 Bypass, Fry Boulevard, Highway 90 and Highway 92.

Because of the increasing numbers, residents in the area had gotten together and decided to name their little community. They offered several ideas but finally reached a consensus: Buena (Spanish for "good"). It stuck. Unfortunately, newer residents who came from places far from the border and unfamiliar with the Spanish language would often pronounce it "B'yew-enna." However, Buena, pronounced correctly, was another name for a part of early Sierra Vista.

About the same time all this was happening, two other momentous events took place. One of them involved the Arizona State Government when, way ahead of the federal authorities, they established statewide prohibition in 1915. The action had unexpected consequences, leading directly to a border confrontation at Naco (south and east of today's Sierra Vista). Because Arizona borders Mexico, problems quickly developed. Many Mexicans wanted to ban alchoholic beverages and, for a while, they were banned in Naco. It didn't matter to most of the residents; there was a lot of bootlegging. As things went, Naco became a well-known watering hole, situated as it was astride the international border. It wasn't that far away, so travel was easily managed. Drinkers didn't want to stay home all the time, so they often met at Naco to celebrate whatever could be celebrated. The situation would continue for a number of years.

A second important thing happened that year. An increasing number of families with children now lived on scattered ranches and in Huachuca Mountain valleys, so the people of Buena decided they needed a school that would go through to the eighth grade. There were small schools here and there, even one in Carr Canyon, but none were consolidated with the ability to take in all the Buena kids.

Buena got their own school, sources say, in the form of an adobe building on land donated by Paul Knoles's great-grandfather, Plimman Hulbert. It was located on the northeast corner of the four-highway intersection, where Target Store and Chili's Restaurant are now. Classes started with the fall semester of 1915 in the adobe school.

There are, however, some discrepancies in describing the school. The late Norine Haverty Dickey described it as having been a store building, matching Paul Knoles's account of his uncle's building on the property, but Dickey says it belonged to a religious group who abandoned it. It's possible; it could have been used, temporarily, by such a group. She also says there were two rooms with a hall between and a potbellied stove in each room. Another historian has described a vaguely different version of the school, describing it only as being the first school

A young 25-year-old Norine Haverty, historian, contributed much information concerning establishment of the Buena School.

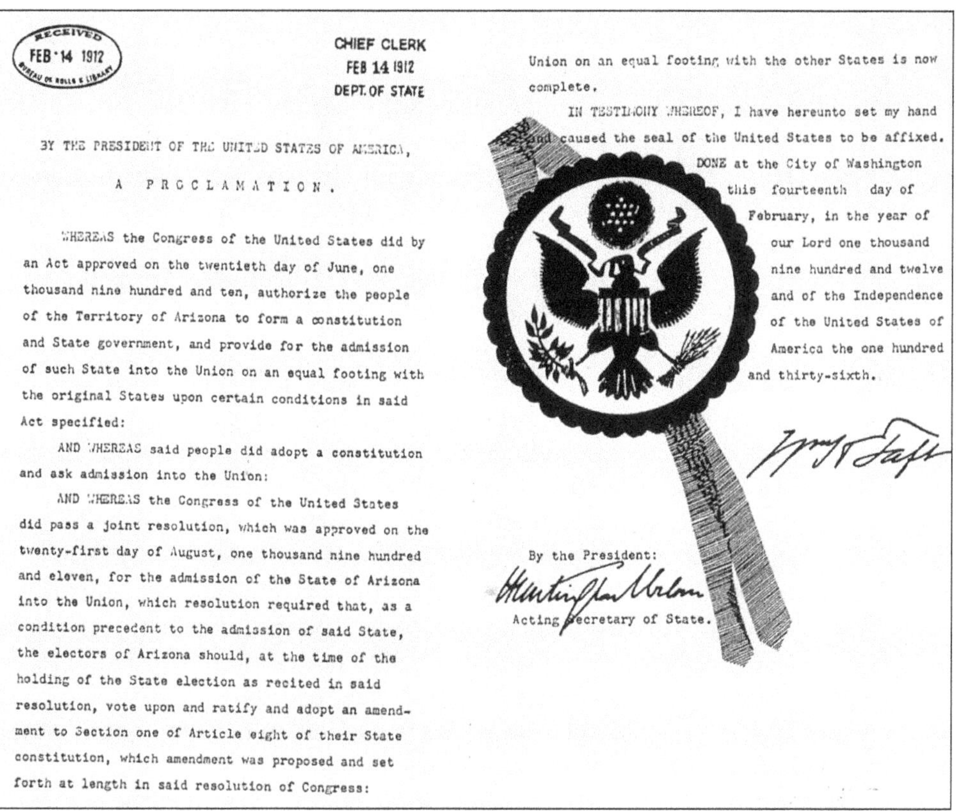

RECEIVED FEB 14 1912 BUREAU OF ROLLS & LIBRARY

CHIEF CLERK
FEB 14 1912
DEPT. OF STATE

BY THE PRESIDENT OF THE UNITED STATES OF AMERICA,

A PROCLAMATION.

WHEREAS the Congress of the United States did by an Act approved on the twentieth day of June, one thousand nine hundred and ten, authorize the people of the Territory of Arizona to form a constitution and State government, and provide for the admission of such State into the Union on an equal footing with the original States upon certain conditions in said Act specified:

AND WHEREAS said people did adopt a constitution and ask admission into the Union:

AND WHEREAS the Congress of the United States did pass a joint resolution, which was approved on the twenty-first day of August, one thousand nine hundred and eleven, for the admission of the State of Arizona into the Union, which resolution required that, as a condition precedent to the admission of said State, the electors of Arizona should, at the time of the holding of the State election as recited in said resolution, vote upon and ratify and adopt an amendment to Section one of Article eight of their State constitution, which amendment was proposed and set forth at length in said resolution of Congress:

Union on an equal footing with the other States is now complete.

IN TESTIMONY WHEREOF, I have hereunto set my hand and caused the seal of the United States to be affixed.

DONE at the City of Washington this fourteenth day of February, in the year of our Lord one thousand nine hundred and twelve and of the Independence of the United States of America the one hundred and thirty-sixth.

Wm H Taft

By the President:

Huntington Wilson

Acting Secretary of State.

This copy of the document granting statehood to the former Territory of Arizona shows the official date of February 14, 1912. (Courtesy of Rosario Guzman.)

and that it opened in the vicinity of a little adobe building north of the railroad tracks, again matching the account of what Knoles remembers as the first school.

A major difficulty in researching this and other buildings is the lack of precise records. Comparatively speaking, Arizona had just recently become a state. It was, in fact, still the "wide open spaces," the "wild west," the frontier. Building permits and the rules governing them didn't exist. You filed on a piece of property or bought it, and then you built on it. Without pictures, the exact year or identifying details may often depend on hand-written notes or possibly just individual memory.

So there is some confusion about Buena School. From all three memoirists and from a few still-living sources, one thing is apparent. There was a "first school" and a "first Buena School." The first Buena School was made of adobe bricks, a fact firmly proven through photography; it was located where Target and Chili's are now. The first Buena School offered classes through the eighth grade but only for a year before another school, with one room, was built. However, this first Buena school building was strong and well built; it stood until the late 1990s and, when it was finally torn down, its bricks were sold as fund-raising collector's items.

At the time, it was only important to have an elementary school, no matter in what form it existed. Buena got a piece of land and they got a building. After obtaining the building, community residents realized there was no storage space; they really needed a basement so they could store winter firewood for the potbellied stove(s). The whole thing would definitely have to be a do-it-yourself project, so the men immediately set to work with picks and shovels. They dug a 4-foot deep basement, putting the small building over it. The floor of the school building would be the roof of the basement. Several feet away from the new school, two outhouses were built, one for the boys and one for the girls.

Though the schoolyard's perimeter was fenced in barbed wire, there was no playground equipment, just marbles or baseball bats and gloves, things some of the kids brought with them. When they played baseball, two lucky boys who owned gloves got to be pitcher and catcher; no one has ever explained whether they played for both teams and thus competed against themselves. There were no buses to pick up the kids and take them to school; students either walked or rode horses, or a buggy, if they had to pick up something on their way home. Once at school, the ones who rode horses had to unsaddle and unbridle the animal (or unhitch it), turn it into the corral, then stash the tack on the porch before going to class. There were no government-mandated hot lunches for the kids (hot lunches didn't appear until the fall semester of 1946); kids usually packed simple cold lunches, maybe just a couple of leftover biscuits, and often brought jugs of water to school with them because of a lack of water on site.

As was customary in those days, a school (or a church) was often the center of social activity. Certainly, Buena School was such a place, and it could qualify under both descriptions, in that a minister preached at the school on Sundays. Because it was a community social hall, a sizeable group was present on Thanksgiving Day, 1915. A photographer snapped a picture of everyone who came to celebrate (thereby proving the building was adobe). In that photo are the kids who would be the next spring's first graduating class (eighth grade) at Buena School. Five students were in that commencement class, four boys and one girl. Alphabetically, they were: Gerald Downer, Edna Fry, Erwin Fry, Dale Mouser, and Charlie Roan. It was a proud day for the youngsters and for their families.

The first teacher at the little adobe schoolhouse, Hazel Whitmore, only lasted through that first year. Deteriorating health forced her termination. Before the second school year began, according to one source, residents of the community decided they needed a different educational facility, so they built a large one-room frame structure nearby and called it Buena School. The first one was abandoned but would resurface in later years. Meanwhile, at the new Buena School, another form of entertainment was available in addition to marbles and baseball and such.

There were two houses within sight of the new school; the second of the two was about a half-mile away, on Fry's property. It was green, with a red light over the door. Living and "working" in the second house was a somewhat infamous woman. The extraordinary, red-haired Hannah Wolfe was a former teacher, highly regarded and respected, who found that the "oldest profession" paid better. All during the school day, students watched as men visited her, coming and going, arriving from nearby ranches or Fort Huachuca. She actually plied two trades, the one formerly mentioned and the retail sale of a certain strong alcoholic beverage. One never knew why a customer came along; it could be for either of the reasons. Unfortunately, they never seemed to notice that kids at the school could see them. The students might giggle; some would become embarrassed at having recognized a visitor because such a one could be a classmate's father or one's own father.

In this way, Buena School had its entertainment. Still, education was its main purpose and when Hazel Whitmore could no longer work, a second teacher was hired. He was a man called Mr. Lewis, but he was suddenly and mysteriously dismissed. He did not quit but was actually dismissed after only a few months. The next teacher at Buena School was Ruby Fulghum, of Willcox, who would go on to be the county's superintendent of schools.

It wasn't long after graduation that a young carpenter from Bisbee came calling at the little convenience store Oliver Fry, the merchant, had established in his small home by partitioning off the boys' bedroom. Charlie Smith was quite taken with the teenaged Edna Fry. Following a suitable courtship, the handsome young carpenter and the pretty milkmaid were married on May 6, 1917. The wedding took place in the Fry home, the ceremony performed by a preacher coming in

On Thanksgiving Day, 1915, a celebration was held at the brand-new adobe Buena School. Paul Knoles, whose relative donated the land on which the school stands, is in about the middle of the front row. (Courtesy of Paul Knoles.)

Halloween at Buena School, nine years later in 1924, shows that there were about 30 students. The teachers were Etoile Parker and Margaret Brimberr. Adult visitors shown here include Harry Wilcox and his wife Mrs. McLaughlin, Mrs. Simmons, and Mrs. Perez. (Courtesy of Mary Estes.)

from Buena. (Likely, it was the same preacher who held services in the Buena School.) The wedding was a real event. Though married couples certainly resided in the community, and weddings may have taken place in villages nearby, the Fry-Smith nuptials were probably the first marriage to take place in Overton, in what would become Fry and, eventually, part of Sierra Vista.

As was expected of him, Charlie made sure he had a home for his new bride. It was in Bisbee, but that was okay. They didn't move right away because Charlie, a carpenter, and his new brother-in-law soon began building a larger adobe house for the Frys. Charlie and Edna stayed there while construction was going on, sleeping at night in a small building nearby on the same property. The arrangement was a model of efficiency, providing the newlyweds some privacy and allowing the men to remain near their construction project while the women shared cooking and laundry facilities. Using the lumber from the original home for the framing of the new one and adobe bricks made by Mexican laborers, it took about four months.

That new house was located where the Family Dollar Store is today. Front and back porches were added, other remodeling done, but it's long been considered "pioneer" construction. Some residents, interested in preserving historic structures, wanted to get it designated as an official historic building. (By the time they got around to doing something, Oliver had died and Oliver's son, Erwin, wouldn't hear of it being anything other than the Fry family home. It was his, and it would never belong to anyone else. It later burned to the ground.)

During the 1920s, the community saw a slight change in people's thoughts about war. World War I had ended a few years earlier. The economy was on the upswing. And, it has been said, some were convinced that if the military establishments were closed, if the soldiers were let go, then America wouldn't get dragged into any more wars. Finally, the War Department decided that the army would be reduced in numbers and prepared a study just in case.

In March 1924, Colonel James Cooper Rhea (post commander at Fort Huachuca) was ordered to estimate the post's value in terms of selling it. He did his research. His report was that the buildings were worth $50,000, installations about $25,000, and land and water systems about $250,000. Fort Huachuca, in 1924, was only worth a total of $325,000. Luckily for Sierra Vista, the army decided to retain Fort Huachuca and closed Fort Apache instead by transferring it to the Indian Service. In fact, at that point Fort Huachuca was the only active army post in the state of Arizona.

The Huachuca Mountains are just outside Sierra Vista. This is but one of the ranges surrounding the community and is an example of the type of terrain that faced the early settlers. (Courtesy of Ron Price.)

6. Incident in the Canyons

The 1920s were known in some parts of the country as the Roaring '20s—not without cause. Even in the new state of Arizona, things were happening. For instance, the railroad had continued building branches; after going to Tombstone in 1903, they built on to Tyrone, New Mexico in 1921. The next year, they merged not only with the Arizona & New Mexico Railroad but also the old Lordsburg & Hatchita Railroad.

After World War I, however, things slowed down and the price of copper dropped. After struggling for a few postwar years, Phelps Dodge figured it was time to regroup, or downsize, and they decided to sell the entire El Paso & Southwestern. Southern Pacific Railroad (SP) offered the munificent sum of $64 million payable in a combination of cash, stock, and bonds. The Interstate Commerce Commission approved and the Southern Pacific took over on November 1, 1924.

(Since that time, substantial track has long since been torn up and the lines discontinued due to mergers and consolidations. Unfortunately, this action left several communities to become ghost towns when former railroad employees left to follow jobs elsewhere. The good part, especially for railroad buffs, is that the SP does still rumble through several towns in southern Arizona.)

It wasn't just the railroads, though. It took some tough, strong-willed people to live on what was basically still the frontier. It was nothing like life east of the Mississippi and especially not like the settled and growing cities on the east coast. Here, a community might consist of two or three family homes in fairly close proximity, one of which might have a shop of some kind on the property. Next, someone might add a little store. Somehow, "town" often included the nearest scattered homes if they were not too many miles away.

For instance, the eastern part of the community down the dirt road from the fort's gate, where the new school existed,was still known as Buena. Closer to the fort's main gate, the western part where the Frys lived, was still called Overton. All of it would eventually blend together to form Sierra Vista.

But this was, as said, still the wild-and-wooly West, where anything could happen. The community was not without its scandals. For instance, a popular and respected Buena-area rancher named Frank Moson, owner of the Y-Lightning

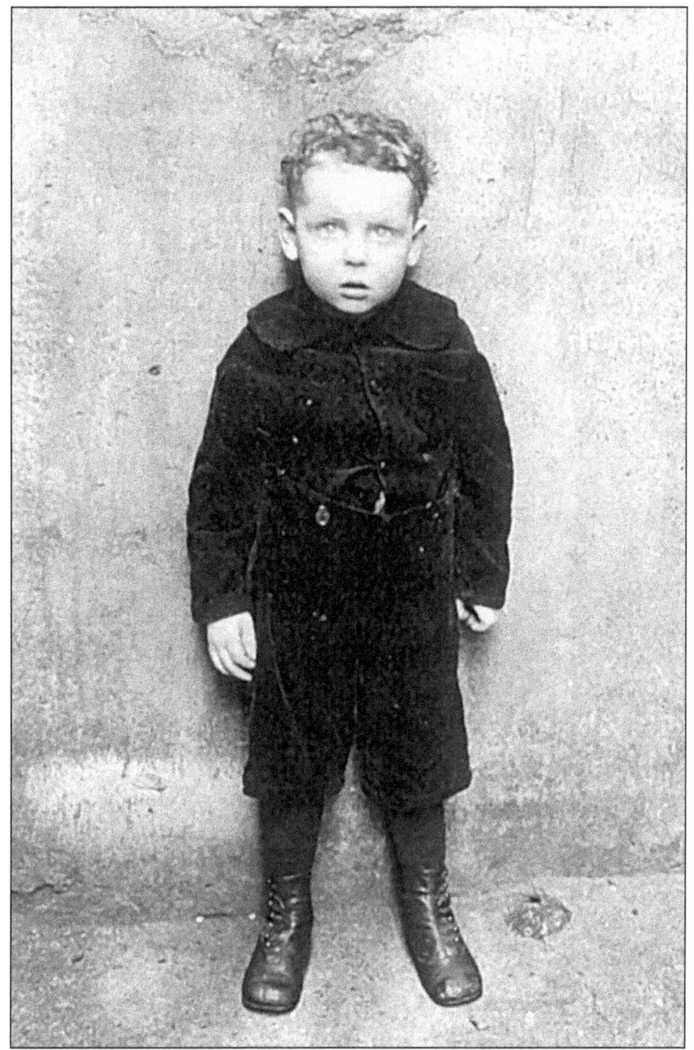

Jimmy Lee is shown here in the 1920s. Jimmy was the eldest son of the railroad man who Mary Persinger married. (Courtesy of the Persinger Collection.)

Ranch, a popular dude ranch, attended the death of a canyon-area man named Haverty. Well, actually both the victim and the offender were named Haverty. They were brothers. The shooting scandalized the entire county and was reported in at least two newspapers, the *Bisbee Daily Review* and the *Tombstone Epitaph*. Moson and his wife would serve as witnesses during the subsequent trial, a matter of public record.

Bad blood had existed between the two brothers from the time they were children, though Jim, the older, had tried to help raise his younger sibling as best he could. Dick seems to have resented his brother's methods, rebelling against his stringent rules and heavy-handed ways. Later, each would threaten to kill the other over various business deals. In the end, it all came down to claims and counterclaims, to mistaken ownership of a bull, and too much temper exacerbated by alcohol. Trouble would erupt when Jim Haverty, in the company of his two sons and a brother-in-law, tried to round up a bull that had gone missing.

Lillian Rice, a teacher, was boarding with Dick and Hortense Haverty, a pair of young newlyweds. Their property was adjacent to and shared borders with that of Dick's brother Jim and Caleb Newman. At various times a constable or other peace officer, Dick was trying to build their own herd while he continued working at Moson's ranch. Each school day, a friend came by to pick up Rice and take her, along with a group of kids, to the school. One Monday, the driver stopped by as usual but noticed that Jim Haverty's kids weren't in the group waiting for her. Rice told her not to wait, the children wouldn't be going to Buena School anymore.

Lillian Rice, who would later become Mrs. Edwin Fry, and her son Jim are shown here in 1919. Jim always thought very highly of his step-father. (Courtesy of the Henry Hauser Museum.)

More than one longtime resident says it all started on Friday when Frank Moson went to visit Dick Haverty, his employee, bringing a quart of tequila and a box of cigars. Moson mentioned that he had an order for a number of steers by a certain date, and Dick replied that there weren't that many head ready for market. According to one source, Moson told Dick that there had better be that many if Dick wanted to keep his job. He further suggested that Jim Haverty's spur brand could easily be modified to look like the Y-Lightning brand that Moson's cattle wore. Without his personal brand on them, Jim wouldn't be able to tell his own cattle from any other. And they kept pouring one drink after another, getting three sheets to the wind and starting to slur their words.

Moson stayed until after midnight. The source says that Lillian Rice told him that when Frank left, Hortense wanted Dick to go to bed and sleep it off but he was determined to go out. What could she do? Only one thing. While kissing him goodbye, she carefully removed his gun from its holster, a gun he was authorized to carry since he was also a peace officer. She handed it to Rice, the teacher. Dick was too drunk to know what was going on. Unarmed, he stumbled out the door.

Early next morning, April 24, Jim Haverty heard cattle bawling as if something was wrong; he woke his sons, Clay and Ellis, to go with him and see what was wrong.

Jim Haverty's testimony was reported verbatim in the *Bisbee Daily Review*:

> . . . it was about 10 o'clock in the morning. I was in my shirt sleeves, and carried a .45 six-shooter in a scabbard with a belt. In driving the bull back to the road, I was on the left and saw a man on horseback coming over the hill. It was Dick Haverty, my brother. I saw we were going to meet and turned the bull to the right in order to miss him.
>
> Dick turned and came to us. He approached us in a circle and dropped in behind. He said to Smith "Hold on; I want to see you," Smith stopped and I went on, but he said "By God, I want to see you too."

Strong curse words were exchanged. Jim continued:

> As he got off his horse, I heard him say "________ you, I will kill you!" As he started off his horse, I started off mine. When I heard him say it, I straightened up on the horse and pulled my six-shooter.
>
> Up to the time he got off his horse, I hadn't seen his right side. He reined his horse with his left hand and his right arm was behind him. I thought he was after his gun when he said "_______ you, I will kill you" and I fired.

After checking his brother to see his condition, Jim Haverty reported, "I said 'I came near leaving my gun at home this morning.' Dick said 'I did leave mine.' "

The *Bisbee Daily Review* also reported that the witness testified that Jim then said "I thought you had it" and Dick answered "You never thought no such thing." Also, the witness added, "After Jim left, Dick said 'I knew me and Jim couldn't get along and I knew something like this was going to happen, and I went off and forgot my gun this morning.' "

More than one witness did say that Dick had told them if he ever caught Jim in his pasture, he'd shoot him in two . . . and if he ever butted into Dick's business, he'd cut Jim [Kelly's] guts out. (Actually, that was threats against two.)

During the trial, many said Dick was a highly respected, peaceful, and law-abiding citizen, that he and his wife Hortense were leaders in Red Cross work. Dick even managed to help keep order during fund-raising dances held at Buena School, keeping bootleggers from making a saloon of the school.

Max Bolding, researching for a national publication, says Lillian Rice offered to tell the court about Frank Moson's visit the night before the shooting, but Jim Haverty didn't think it would be a good idea to get Moson mixed up in it. He advised her to say nothing. His sons told Lillian and Hortense to keep quiet when questioned; Jim's mother, Amanda, asked him not to say or do anything that would besmirch Dick's good name.

The trial proceeded, with up to 49 character witnesses telling what they knew of the lifelong feud between the brothers. The biggest disagreement came over the exact wording of Dick Haverty's dying statement. One witness, not to the shooting but to the dying statement, said he understood Dick to say, "I threw up my hands and fell down when he shot me." The other version, the one taken down in writing by Frank Moson, with witnesses' signatures, had Dick saying "When he threw down on me, I threw up my hands and he shot me." The statements seem almost identical but in court, there's a big difference.

The trial went on. On August 17, the courthouse in Tombstone hosted an unexpected bit of high drama. In the courtroom, supported by friends, the young widow listened to a description of her husband's shooting, saw the bloody shirt he wore when he was killed, listened to character witnesses both for and against. She listened as witnesses admitted her late husband always carried a gun and that anyone would expect it to be no different on the day of the shooting. And she surely must have remembered that she'd taken Dick's gun from him, that she was responsible for his being unarmed that morning. His brother testified that Dick's right arm was behind him; had he been reaching for his gun? Dick didn't know it was missing. If she had not taken the gun, would a different brother be sitting in the courtroom? Did she help cause her husband to be killed?

Whatever thoughts swirled through her head, Hortense Haverty managed to hold up until the 16th. First, the parties tried to have her removed from the courtroom; Judge Lockwood decided, after hearing arguments, that she could stay. She did, but eventually reached her limits. According to newspaper reports on August 17, she "broke down" during testimony about the bloody shirt as it was exhibited, with the bullet hole still in it, for the jury to see. In the packed room, all eyes turned to the lady in widow's weeds as she sobbed bitterly. Later, as they were leaving the courtroom, each with their own escorts, the widow and the accused passed in the hall. A few feet past him, nearly to the door, Hortense abruptly turned and ran back after her brother-in-law. Drawing back, putting all her strength into it, she gave him a resounding slap in the face. Bursting into tears, she was pulled away from Jim by attorneys and friends.

His cheek stinging from her attack, Jim Haverty reacted with strong words; a heated exchange ensued. On the one hand, the defendant was on the receiving end of Hortense's justifiably emotional and very public outburst. On the other, her supporters objected to his alleged treatment of the young widow. That "treatment," they felt, was an added cruelty that she simply could not bear. When authorities asked why she had done it, she explained that Jim Haverty had looked at her sneeringly in the courtroom, all during the trial. Then, she said, when they passed in the corridor, he leered in her face. There is no record that anyone asked her to explain what she meant by "sneeringly" and "leered."

James Haverty would be found guilty not of murder, but of manslaughter. He was given the maximum sentence, 10 years.

Haverty had remained relatively calm throughout the trial. Even at announcing of the sentence, he appeared unmoved. It wasn't until he was back in jail that he grew moody and morose, refusing to see his friends or allow them to see him. He grew angrier and angrier, getting into a loud argument with his attorney. He demanded that his attorney ask for a new trial. It didn't happen.

In the aftermath, Lessie Mae, Jim's wife, and the children moved away. Dick's murder was built into a crime of such proportions that if a child named Haverty showed up, people whispered; they joked about who was going to get killed. It made life for the kids very difficult. And rumors were rife.

Cattle shared—and still share—their space with wildlife such as these deer, an example of canyon life in the mid-1920s. (Courtesy of Ron Price.)

One such rumor was that a bunch of Moson's cowboys threw branded cowhides into an old well on Jim's property. Another is that someone deposited money in a bank, payable to Jim's lawyer if he was sent to prison. (Jim was warned in time; he could have fired the lawyer and gotten another, but he didn't listen.) And he did go to prison, yet he didn't serve the entire ten years.

On August 23, 1926, he was paroled and walked out of the Florence prison a free man. Yet he wasn't entirely free. For his children's sake, Jim sold his ranch to Bill Carmichael, then moved to Tempe. Alice Higgins, the boys' teacher, knew Jim was a trustee at Buena School. In a snit with the Havertys over a very different matter, she made use of the scandal and blamed one of the boys for everything that happened. Lessie Mae, Jim's wife, divorced him after he got out of prison. No one in the family wanted to talk about the whole incident, it was too painful and they hoped it would be forgotten.

It could have been, and was, swept under the rug. But nothing that is a matter of public record, that has been reported in more than one newspaper or researched by someone like Max Bolding, can ever be completely forgotten.

Ranchland surrounded what would become Sierra Vista. (Courtesy of the Henry Hauser Museum.)

7. How Community Names Evolved

Perhaps that bottle of tequila consumed the night before the Haverty shooting came from a bar in nearby Naco, perhaps from a bootlegger. Its source doesn't matter. The fact is, Naco had enjoyed its reputation as a watering hole for a number of years. It was soon to become a player in another very "western" event.

Religious problems developed between the president of Mexico and the Roman Catholic Church, resulting in persecuted priests actually closing down all the churches in Mexico. (The president of Mexico did not like the priests having influence over the people. Missions were raided, services interrupted, materials destroyed, and priests captured and beaten or killed.) Rebellion ensued. Crops were destroyed, transportation interrupted, water sources rendered unusable. More than two dozen nuns managed to escape across the border, and many of the faithful were forced to attend services on the American side, in Arizona. It couldn't last.

The rebellions were taking place throughout Mexico, more so away from the northern regions. However, a group led by one Jose Escobar developed the Plan of Hermosillo and began a northern rebellion in 1928. First, they took over Cananea. High on their success, knowing that by taking (and holding) Agua Prieta and Naco, they would have enough money to keep fighting for a long time, they forged ahead. Early the next year, in 1929, they made it to Naco where a large number of sympathizers were on their side.

Considerate? Maybe they were. They later claimed it was a gesture of good will towards the American customers (and perhaps to make sure more money was in the tills), when the rebels waited till late evening to attack. Beginning in late March 1929, their operation began at 8 p.m. Choosing a favorite tactic, they quietly appropriated an untended rail car, then filled it with dynamite before sending it whizzing along the tracks, heading straight for the center of the city. There was no engineer, no guidance system in use, and the tracks were not perfectly straight. It was a disaster waiting to happen, and happen it did, although before reaching the more populated downtown. The car derailed, its load of dynamite exploded, and the resulting fire destroyed whatever remained; however, by crashing where it did, an even more terrible disaster was averted. Most buildings at the time were some form of dry wood, adobe (a mixture of dried mud and straw), or a combination of the two. Such materials burn incredibly fast and there was a lack of firefighting equipment (often a simple bucket-brigade was the only thing available); it often meant entire city blocks burned to the ground. Therefore, the rebels' ineptness meant collateral damage was kept to a minimum, and property and innocent lives were saved.

That first attempt failed, but the rebels were not about to give up. What they needed was reinforcements. They found a crop duster named Patrick Murphy and the government hired another pilot named Jon Gorre. Along with a small group of other pilots, all soldiers of fortune, they had airplanes that could carry explosives. Murphy had earlier been in trouble with the law but that didn't matter; he could deliver what the rebels wanted. And his bombs, while crude, would be effective. They were made from dynamite mixed with scrap iron, nails, bolts, and similar damaging items, which were then stuffed into ordinary suitcases or a five-gallon gasoline can; then a strip-fuse was attached (a form of Molotov Cocktail before the term was invented).

According to a witness, Murphy and Gorre took turns attacking. One would fly around and bomb the enemy, a.k.a. the rebels; when he landed, the other would take a turn, intending to bomb the Federales. The late Charlie Elledge was, at the time, working for the Southern Pacific Railway. (He would later own a Western Auto Store on the main drag of pre-Sierra Vista, about where Sun 'n' Spokes is now.) When it all started, he was repairing the roof of the immigration building on the American side. This gave him an excellent vantage point. When the fracas began, the rebels, led by General Escobar, had a camp just south of the border but the Federales had recaptured Naco. The rebels needed help. Enter the pilots.

Charlie said both pilots used the same kind of bombs, buying them from the same guy. It got kind of messy, too, because the pilots' aim didn't seem all that good; neither appeared to be a "Dead-Eye Dick." Of course, the usual late spring/early summer wind was a contributing factor. And it surprised many that when the two planes landed for the day, the pilots were good friends, going off to celebrate with a few drinks. Then the following day they were back up there, flying and bombing for opposing sides. Some historians have erroneously described the action as if both pilots were flying for the same bosses, playing on the same team. They weren't. Both were hired by Mexicans, but for opposing sides. Most folk of the day didn't really know which was which.

First, Murphy tried two runs that were unproductive duds. The next bomb found a target. One source says it was by another pilot, probably Gorre, and one says it was Murphy's third run before he managed to hit anything. Regardless, when the first bomb exploded, the bars and clubs on the Mexican side of Naco quickly emptied as all the American customers made a beeline back across the border to Naco, Arizona. Residents of Bisbee joined them. Charlie Elledge admitted that his job gave him a top-notch view of the action; he also said that up to 200 people would gather to watch, even climbing on top of stationary

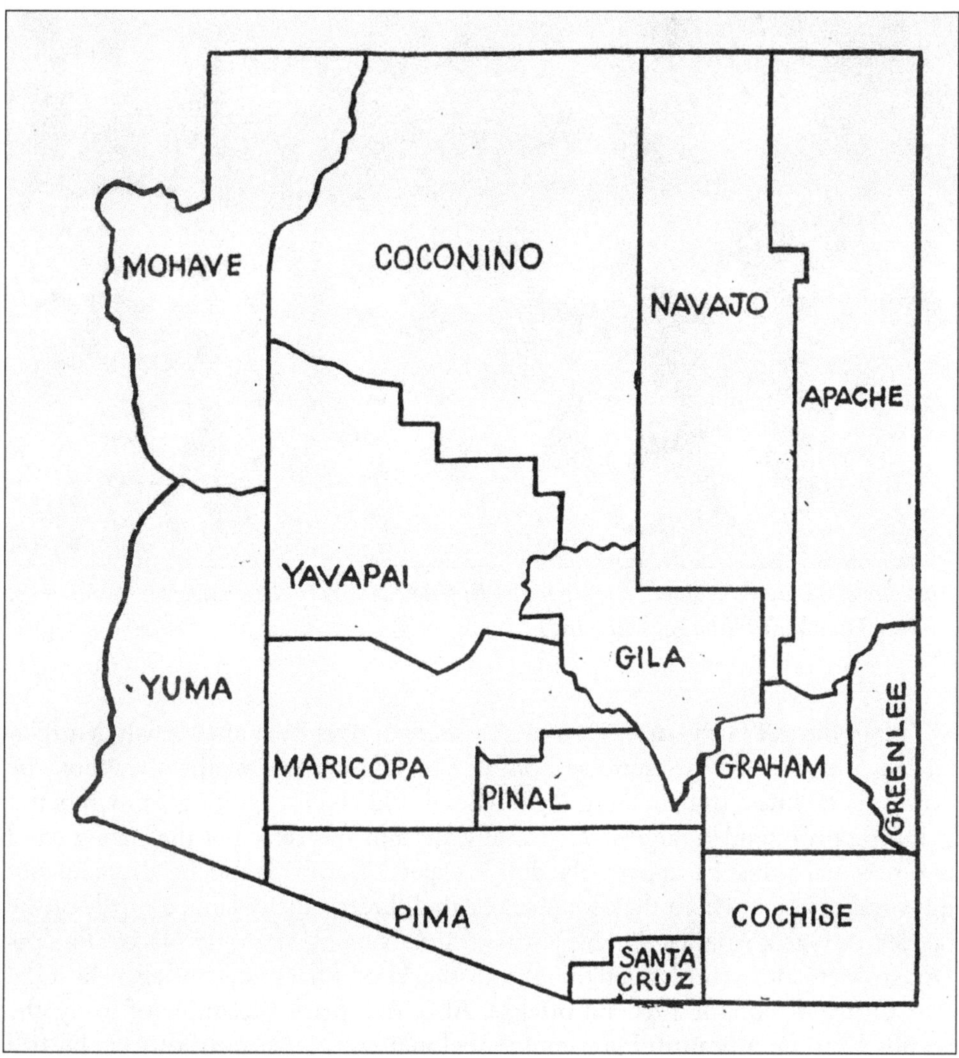

This map shows the location of Cochise County in relation to the state of Arizona. The southernmost border is shared with Mexico.

rail cars for a better view, treating the whole situation as if it were a sideshow, a celebration, or an unexpected fireworks display. Men, women, and entire families brought food, packing well-stocked picnic baskets, and chatted excitedly, making bets about where the next bomb would land. When the flying soldiers of fortune finally hit something—a customhouse on that third run—the resulting explosion sprayed a few of the spectators with small bits of building materials and other shrapnel. A visiting photographer and a reporter were hit. There were minor injuries, but none of the spectators were killed. Finally realizing their danger, the party on the American side broke up. Everyone went home, some of them to Overton/Fry and Buena.

This photo, dated 1890, shows a company of Buffalo Soldiers in dress uniform. (Courtesy of the Fort Huachuca Historical Museum.)

Things did get a little more serious. A couple of days later, after lunch, Murphy loaded four more of his suitcase bombs. On his first run of the afternoon, he dropped one into a trench, killing two federal soldiers. He didn't get much better at hitting his intended targets. Technically, his aim was okay but the strong wind is a seasonal thing he apparently didn't expect. Bombs could be dropped but the wind affected where they touched earth. Three actually landed north of the border, in Naco, Arizona. He hit a garage and damaged not only Naco's Phelps-Dodge Mercantile (no longer there) and the Haas Pharmacy, but also the U.S. Post Office, making it a federal offense. Also, in a perfect example of irony, the bombs blew up a beautiful automobile belonging to a Mexican officer; he had stored it on the American side for safekeeping.

Whether Murphy or Gorre (who died in 1980) ever got paid is unknown; rumor has it that they didn't. However, one man made quite a lot of money. That's because, during the fracas, the No. 11 passenger train pulled into Naco carrying silver to pay the federal troops stationed there. Each soldier got two pesos for each day on duty. All of them were poor, some without shoes, and the instant they got their hands on the money, they ran across the border to Harry Block's store and bought everything he had.

The small Naco conflict was, unfortunately, an international incident. Although most damage was done on the Mexican side of the border and the major participants were Mexican, it also did damage on the U.S. side of the border. On the other hand, bombing runs were made by American mercenaries hired by Mexicans. So when bombs landed on the American side, it could have gotten really sticky. Actually, the day after the ill-conceived bombing runs, Mexican federal troops moved in while Murphy was doing some loop-de-loops and other aerial acrobatics, showing off, laughing and taunting the officials. Federal troops shot his plane more than 30 times. It coasted to the ground, Murphy still alive inside. Disabled, the plane could do no more damage to either side.

Surprisingly and for unknown reasons, Federales did not arrest him. Murphy simply laid low till the fracas was over, then crossed the border back to the United States. There he was immediately arrested by the Americans.

However, the rebellion didn't end with Murphy's third run. The Mexican rebels were determined and Gorre's plane was not grounded. On April 3, 1929, they managed to drop a few more bombs. In doing so, they blasted out a big crater on the American side of the border, but no one was injured. Three days later, on April 6, the rebels tried to come into Naco behind some appropriated tanks that ran interference. It didn't work and they retreated to Cananea by way of Agua Prieta. (The bombing runs at Naco were, by the way, the only time the mainland United States has been bombed by a foreign power.)

The Americans finally had enough. Luckily, although the government had closed all other army posts in Arizona that year, they kept Fort Huachuca open. The fort was relatively close to Naco, so they sent two companies of Buffalo Soldiers into Naco, Arizona. Once there, it didn't take long to pitch tents and set up camp on a hill just north of the border. Actually, they bivouacked just about

This photo, dated 1910, shows a group of Buffalo Soldiers playing craps in the barracks, definitely against the rules. They kept a guard at the door just in case. (Courtesy of the Fort Huachuca Historical Museum.)

where the Turquoise Valley Golf Course—oldest in the state—is today. The site gave them a good view of the surrounding area, especially that across the border.

While the regular troops were going about their business, the officer in charge looked around, investigated the bombed-out crater and, since no one was injured, said, "Well, dirt is cheap." That wasn't disrespectful; it simply was a way to acknowledge the value of dirt versus human life. It didn't mean he was going to back off or let the battles continue raining unwarranted damage on this side of the border. He chose decisive action. Carrying a white flag as he crossed the Arizona/Sonora border, he rode to meet with the leader of the rebel troops. He said in no uncertain terms that they would stop bombing the United States, or the next thing they heard would be his bugler sounding "Charge!" The cavalry troops and the bugler were fully prepared and ready to go, waiting only for his command to ride across the border and wipe them out. The officer made a good argument.

It is rumored that General Escobar, the Mexican rebel leader, had stashed an airplane somewhere after first loading it with gold. When he saw the futility of his war, he more or less abandoned his troops and took off in the plane, landing somewhere in the United States. There, he asked for and received asylum

Meanwhile, that same month, the Haverty trial certainly electrified the citizens in this particular corner of Cochise County. When it was finally over, Lillian Rice, the teacher who boarded with Dick and Hortense Haverty and who offered to testify at Jim's trial, would mount her personal war before going on to become very important in the history of Sierra Vista. The first thing she did was to launch

This image shows another view of the original Carmichael Store, now the Daisy Mae Steakhouse. (Courtesy of the Henry Hauser Museum.)

a four year campaign to get rid of all the little green shacks with red lights over the door. They seemed to grow exponentially along the road from Garden Canyon/ Fry/Overton to Buena.

Not everyone was happy with her efforts. It was true that prostitutes caused the spread of disease, but residents could also buy moonshine from them (a big selling point during prohibition). Merchants and farmers sold vegetables or dairy products to them. Even the popular dude ranches and tourist attractions of that era liked having the cathouses around. Because it contributed to the rowdy, freewheeling "Western" atmosphere described in paperback literature of the time, owners of such ranches actually encouraged the proliferation of such establishments. It was, for them, a definite tourist draw. Oliver Fry was another who wasn't crazy about Rice's campaign. After all, he owned the Garden Canyon Store, the post office, the garage, and the bakery, and the prostitutes gave him plenty of business. He also owned the row of houses where these women plied their trade, and he collected quite a bit of rent from them.

On the other hand, the more respectable women of the town and the ranchers' wives were firmly on the side of Rice. Their husbands, however, took up the case and convinced them that the hookers were necessary. If the bordellos weren't there, the men argued, if the prostitutes weren't allowed to do business, the Negro soldiers out at Fort Huachuca would be uncontrollable, rampaging through town and attacking the "good women" of the community. In fact, there was no telling what they might do! Strangely, it never occurred to those women to question why their husbands never said the same of the other soldiers. Or why the African-American soldiers were any different from local men who gathered at the nearest speakeasy.

Still, the teacher whittled away at what she considered a sinful blight on the landscape. She didn't manage everything she set out to do. She didn't "clean the slate," but she did get all brothels within a mile of Buena School removed. There would be only one that could even be seen from the schoolyard.

Rice and her husband also got a divorce. There is no information about Mr. Rice, but she was married and they had a child. She apparently came west without her spouse. For awhile, Rice's little boy visited his mother in summer, when school was out. After she remarried, her son came to live with her and her new husband.

Throughout her attempts to clean up the community, Erwin Fry (son of Oliver Fry) encouraged Rice; in fact, he was her devoted assistant. Perhaps even then he had his eye on the comely and spirited teacher because, after her divorce from Mr. Rice, Fry began a serious courtship that culminated in marriage. Their home was quarters behind the Garden Canyon Store, leased from the Carmichaels. It is now Daisy Mae's Steakhouse.

It was quite a year. There were the Naco incident and the Haverty trial. When it was over and Jim Haverty paroled, it was about time for another blip on the radar screen of history. It was called the Great Depression, and the people of Cochise County did not escape its effects.

Countywide, the 1930 census showed 40,998. It would drastically drop because, along with the Depression, the price of copper dropped and most of Arizona's copper mines closed down. Those that didn't close trimmed production to the bare minimum. In 1929, according to the Historical Atlas of Arizona, Arizona produced over 830 million pounds (415,000 tons!), but within two years, production had dropped to 182 million (only 91,000 tons), a drop of substantially more than 75 percent. Although these are statewide figures, it's important to remember that a lot of the Fry/Buena/Sierra Vista income was derived, either directly or indirectly, from the copper mines in Bisbee and the silver mines in Tombstone. There were the ranches, of course, but the purpose of a ranch is to sell beef. Without money, sales slowed. There were the railroads, but without copper or silver or beef to haul, the rail business dropped as well. Without income, customers buy less of everything, so the merchants lose out. Some of them had to close their doors completely.

Paul Knoles tells how his family lost everything. They came to Cochise County to grow watermelons and other produce. When that didn't exactly work the way they planned, Paul's father, an entrepreneur, started a bakery that was quite successful. Unfortunately, a nearby carpentry shop stored a 50 gallon barrel of turpentine on the premises, and the barrel exploded. The bakery and carpentry shop were in a series of old wooden buildings that burned quickly. Paul remembers, "It was the night I graduated from high school."

The fire was a setback, but it didn't keep them down for long. His father borrowed money from four banks to build another store. The Knoleses were on the upswing, doing well, baking for Tombstone, delivering bread to Willcox, Benson, Bisbee, Douglas, and probably points in between. The buyers could afford it because miners were paid good money, as much as $12 a week. Of course, that didn't matter a whit after the value of silver declined and the mines had to shut down.

Times were hard and there was little in the way of comfort from attending religious services. It wasn't until after the Stock Market Crash of 1929 that a Catholic parish was established in southeast Arizona. When it did, it was in Benson in 1930. A resident priest was assigned there but the towns in the surrounding countryside—including Fry—were mere missions of that parish. In a perfect example of cooperation, non-military people, single or in families, could attend religious services at one of the Fort Huachuca chapels, a practice in effect until the post was deactivated in the late 1940s.

When the post was deactivated and the chapels no longer in use, the Fry area reverted to mission status based out of Benson. Fry had no priest assigned them, relying on any who cared to visit. Consequently, Catholic services were often held in private homes and, because there was no church, Mrs. Henry Jones (a resident of Fry) was caretaker of "all sacred things" to include linens, candles, etc.

Times were tough and about to get tougher. In a sort of ripple effect, one business failure led to another. People moved away. (Fort Huachuca, however, did increase their military personnel in 1933, the 25th Infantry relocating two

This image shows branding day at the ranch. Roy Wilcox is holding the calf's head down, while Walter Wilcox is in the background looking for the next one. The other men are unidentified. (Courtesy of the Henry Hauser Museum.)

battalions to the fort. And the 10th Cavalry—the Buffalo Soldiers—were still there. It just wasn't enough to keep all those businesses afloat.)

Another blow to the bakery came when the county courthouse moved from Tombstone to Bisbee, the county seat. With that one move, the Knoleses lost $30 a day in business. Not a lot of money now, but it was a significant amount at the time. Then, the Tombstone silver mines closed down and the Bisbee copper mines curtailed production. The triple whammy killed off most of the bakery's business. The final straw was when, without customers, even the bank went broke and closed! So there they were, with a family to feed and no money, everything lost.

However, the Knoles family were not like some executives in cities back east who panicked and jumped out the windows to their deaths; no, the Knoleses were of sturdier stock. The family, like many others, pulled up their roots. It was

This view of the Carmichael Store shows non-mechanized transportation waiting patiently. (Courtesy of the Henry Hauser Museum.)

during these years that county population dropped from 40,998 in 1930 to 34,627 in 1940. Paul relocated temporarily; it was a long time for temporary, but years later, he would return to the community where his great-uncle donated a little adobe building as the very first schoolhouse for the kids of Buena.

Yes, families managed to survive the Depression, tightening their belts to the last notch. A joke at the time is that if you were at the end of your rope, you simply tied a knot in the end and held on. Somehow, a lot of tough Arizonans survived. Often at the near end of their rope, they "tied the knot" through hard work and making do. They held on.

It helped if they worked on the army post. In 1932, the army needed a dairyman. There was actually a 40-acre farm on the post. It wasn't self-supporting but it did supply vegetables, cattle, milk, and such to the approximately 1,100 troops stationed there. Heeding the call, Leo Schrader left his own dairy farm near Phoenix and moved his family to Fort Huachuca. They managed the farm, which included milk cows, pigs, chickens, rabbits, pack animals, cavalry mounts, and the draft horses used to pull the farm equipment.

The complexity of managing the farm grew. Besides looking after all the animals, they grew corn and alfalfa to feed the animals. Everything produced—plant and animal—was sold at the PX Dairy.

The Schraders did an excellent job, and the army farm, which had never before earned its keep, began to show a profit. In a win-win situation, the pigs thrived on the army's garbage, then in a sort of 360-degree turn, they supplied the troops (until a new commanding officer decided that pigs shouldn't be near a dairy). In fact, by 1936, the Schraders had the army farm up and running well. Without a challenge, Leo felt it was time to change jobs. He quit the management job and established his own farm just about where the East Gate is now.. He bought a place not far off what is now Highway 90, just northeast of the intersection. Schrader Road was named for the family and leads right into the property where he built his own farm. Four years later, Leo moved again when the army decided to enlarge Fort Huachuca, but he maintained his ties to the post because he still outbid everyone else for the garbage that he, in turn, fed his pigs.

In town, there was a little store built by the Carmichaels, also housing a small post office. Because it was built near where gardens supplied produce to feed the troops, Garden Canyon became the name used by the railroad as a destination; thus, the railroad actually gave the community its first official name. Although the town was also called Overton for a short while (that's what it was called when the Haverty Trial electrified everyone), the name just didn't seem to stick. Sometimes a name evolves from a comment, such as "I gotta go to Overton's," then later the possessive is dropped. That may have been the case with the name Overton because there was a man by that name who ran an auto and carriage shop. Unfortunately, very few people seem to recall it. They do remember Garden Canyon and Fry.

David Santor writes in *The History of the Sierra Vista Police Department* that Oliver Fry succeeded Bill Carmichael as postmaster. When he did, says Santor, he put the name Fry on the building. Thereafter, incoming mail was sent to "Fry, Arizona." It is said that on April 1, 1937, the name of the town was changed to Fry; whether it was an official name change or whether it simply evolved is not certain at this point.

Another source claims that Lillian Fry had been working in the grocery-cum-post office and when she was appointed postmaster in 1938, the ambitious Frys didn't renew their lease on the Carmichael Store. It would cause a rift in the relationship between the two families. In the meantime, the Frys put up a new store and more or less took the post office with them because Lillian was postmaster. Then—as owners are often wont to do—they simply named the new building by putting their name on it. The upshot of their action caused the post office to take on the name of Fry with the surrounding community evolving into Fry as well.

It is possible that both are correct if the name of the town is truly tied to the establishment of a post office. Prior to 1930, there was a different procedure for establishing a post office than there was after 1930. The procedure to name an official postmaster involved several steps; there was the nomination, the confirmation of that nomination, the dated signing of the papers and the mailing thereof, and the date that the postmaster assumed his/her duties. Even the official records are not consistent as to establishment dates, but most tend to use the date papers were signed and mailed. So it's possible that dates someone was the official postmaster and dates that same someone was, to all intents and purposes, the local postmaster don't always match.

In the late 1930s, Arizona was still in the toddlerhood of being a state, and this wasn't an incorporated town; it lacked the strict controls of today. Precise to-the-day records weren't always kept, so everyone may know what happened but exact dates can be rather difficult. Adding to the confusion, a new store, according to Jim Rice, Mrs. Fry's son, was quickly put up in 1934, with the post office in it.

At this point, conflicting dates include 1934, 1937, and 1938. The one thing all sources agree upon is that the Frys did move out of the Carmichael Store on Garden Avenue after being there for ten years, and that they built their own store, taking the post office with them. They agree on the approximate location (just west of Fifth Street, where Las Casitas Restaurant is now). They agree that Oliver and Lillian placed the name "Fry" prominently on the outside of the new building. All perfectly legal and well within their rights, of course, but since it's also the custom to put a community's name on a train stop, it caused the railroad to start bringing mail to "Fry, Arizona."

Add 1936 to that list of possible years for the building of a store and the subsequent name change. Why? Because another respected source firmly states that it was 1936 when Erwin Fry and his wife, Lillian Rice Fry, moved out of the store they had leased from the Carmichaels. The Frys moved, this source says, because they built their own store.

They stayed in that new spot for quite a long while. People remember it being there. Just the date it was started is in question. Kathy Mayo, who wasn't yet born when it was built, remembers the store still being there several years later. She says of those later years:

> When I was a little kid, my Mom shopped there. I played marbles in the dirt yard in front of that store; to me, it had been around forever! The outside was white and it had big windowsills that I could climb up on and look in. Chickens scratched around in the front. All the little kids hung out there while their parents shopped, so we got to play together. We looked forward to it.

Meanwhile, it was the late 1930s, and the rumbling of troubles in Europe grew louder and louder. The coming war would, in a circuitous way, twice affect population and business in the southeast corner of Cochise County. When Fort Huachuca expanded, it meant additional support services, not only on the post but also in town. The post was self-sufficient, if need be, but soldiers and their families liked to come into town. Having a small village clustered on the post's doorstep was great. It was just a little community that started as a few homesteads before growing into a "stringtown," but it was there and it was definitely on the move. As of yet though, it really was short on entertainment facilities, yet the town gave the troops and their families a little respite from military life.

That little town had already tried several names—White City, Garden Canyon, Overton, Fry, and earlier on, a couple of others that are more obscure. In fact, a few claims that Sierra Vista had once been known by such-and-such a name is not exactly true. According to some maps, said names were actually used somewhere in the vicinity of the town, maybe an expanded homestead in a nearby canyon (which may not have been too "nearby" depending on how one defines the term). Such outlying communities were usually gone before Sierra Vista existed, before it grew out to meet them. Any claim that they were a former name of Sierra Vista exists because the city has since grown to where it takes in territory that was such a place.

It was, however, still called Fry in the late 1930s and early 1940s, and Buena was just down the road. More importantly, Fry and Buena would eventually join together to become Sierra Vista.

Allegedly the oldest homestead in Cochise County, this structure still stands and is located on Cochise Stronghold Road. (Courtesy of Ron Price.)

8. After the Great Depression

Some of the upswing in the local economy was, admittedly, due to the military; all through the winter of 1938, a new base housing area was under construction. It involved using stone quarried from the Huachuca Canyon creek bed, the same area where Captain Whitside first established the post back in 1877. The project was, for the times, a rather expensive undertaking but one deemed necessary. The new houses were built for the Non-Commissioned Officers (NCOs) and their families, then the Works Progress Administration (WPA) built a reservoir not far from the original one on Reservoir Hill. Water, whether for drinking or laundry and anything in between, was actually hard to find. So, in addition to the reservoirs, several deep wells were dug.

Although the army often uses its own manpower, construction projects on the magnitude of this one can involve outside contractors. In this case, it did exactly that, beginning in the latter part of the Depression. Several new jobs were created under the WPA program. Trailer courts came into being, along with "tent cities" and several units that couldn't be called anything other than shacks. Some of the workers were local; others came from widely scattered parts of the United States and stayed. In a short time, school enrollment grew from 35 to 450. Classrooms were overflowing, bursting at the seams. New businesses opened. More soldiers arrived at Fort Huachuca, spending their off-time (and money) in Fry.

The low rumbling in Europe grew louder; soon it would become a war and local history would be forever changed. For one thing, the army became more modern. It could no longer operate like it did during the confrontation in Naco and earlier. It would no longer be a company or two of mounted cavalry, riding out on horseback to quell this uprising or put down that disturbance. Previously, the post had been a comparatively (by today's standards) small frontier outpost; until late 1940, the fort never could brag of even a full regiment of infantry troops. That year, however, the 1st Battalion, 25th Infantry was activated, modified, and became the nucleus of a complete, full-size regiment. Troops from six states—across the Midwest and East Coast—were assigned to Fort Huachuca, bringing the total presence at the base to the largest it ever had been—5,500 men! Of course, it affected Fry and Buena. Even Bisbee, Lowell, San Jose, Hereford

This image shows the neighborhood in the making. More people meant more homes were needed. (Courtesy of the Henry Hauser Museum.)

(which, by the way, is not where it started), Camp Stone (now Huachuca City), and several more small communities nearby felt the effects of the population increase.

The early 1940s were different in Fry in several ways. Tension was high. No one knows if it contributed to some of the more bizarre events. For instance, one year saw the hanging of two men (for separate crimes) at Fort Huachuca—the only time it ever happened out there, never before and never since. The first incident involved only a couple of soldiers but resulted from drinking and fighting. The second sentence was carried out after a killing that directly involved a woman who lived in Fry.

In 1942, Hazel Craig (her married name) was a woman who oozed a certain type of appeal, very attractive (today, we would say sexy), a woman who liked bright lights, loud music, and having a good time. She liked it when a man spent money on her and wasn't above playing one suitor against another.

That year, Hazel regularly dated the young post librarian, Staff Sergeant Jerry Sykes, who was clearly smitten with her. Unfortunately, even his regular-as-clockwork monthly paycheck that he apparently spent mostly on her wasn't enough once Hazel laid eyes on another soldier named Lester Craig. She now had bigger fish to fry. Suddenly, the man with the unglamorous job as a librarian wasn't so exciting. First of all, Sergeant Craig outranked Sykes, which gave him a bigger paycheck and more authority. Hazel was impressed, and she married Lester Craig. After their wedding, Lester and Hazel continued living in Fry while she, certain of her power, played a most dangerous game. She kept Sykes wrapped around her finger. Although she was now married to someone else, Sykes kept spending most of his paycheck on her. Whether Sergeant Craig knew of his wife's prior relationship with Sykes, he accepted it as a part of her past, apparently unaware of the current state of affairs. Incredibly, each of the two men still called the other his friend. Trouble was definitely brewing, and it boiled over on June 22, 1942.

That night, the Craigs were hosting a party where hard liquor would be plentiful. Sykes was invited, and arrived about 8 p.m. expecting the usual good time. There would be plenty of hard liquor and, he anticipated, time for a little personal interaction with Mrs. Craig. He wasn't expecting the news Hazel was going to deliver. Her husband, recently promoted to first sergeant, was getting a bigger paycheck. Hazel Craig really didn't need Sykes's money anymore. Exciting as the game had been, it was increasingly chancy and more than a little dangerous. She decided to end their relationship. She planned to tell him that night, sometime during the party, that it was over between them.

Perhaps a little afraid, she waited. Several guests arrived at the party, and when it turned out the Craigs didn't have enough liquor, Hazel and a girlfriend went

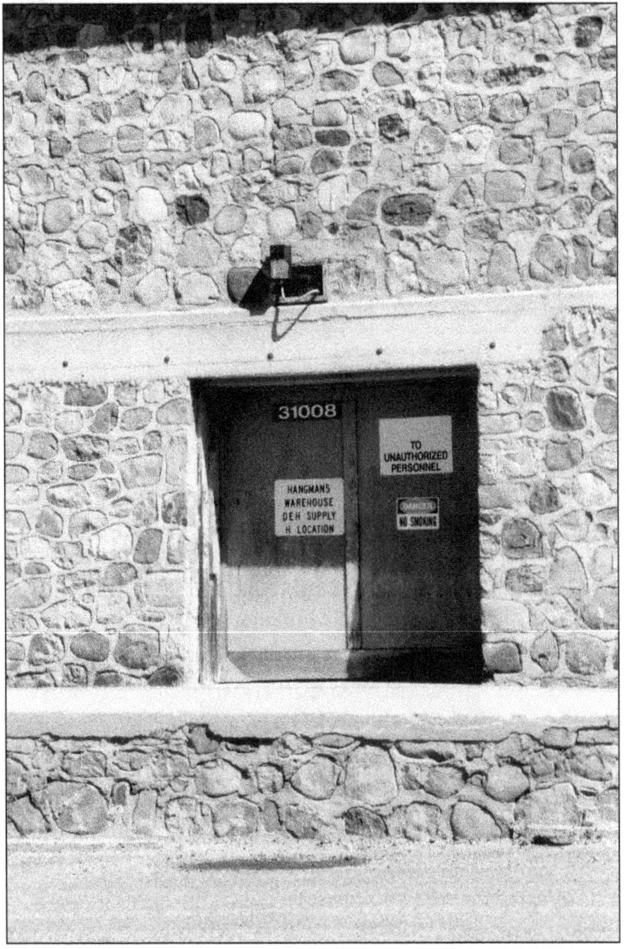

This image shows the entrance to the "Hangman's Warehouse," Building 31008, *at Fort Huachuca. It is part of the historic old fort and can still be viewed by the public. (Courtesy of Ron Price.)*

to a nearby store for more. Maybe she had already dropped the bombshell on Sykes, or maybe not. Regardless, the noisy party continued during the women's absence, leaving Sykes to wander unrestricted around the home. No one paid attention to him, and no one noticed as he stepped through the door and into the kitchen. Once there, he puttered around, finding the usual assortment of sharp knives. Looking them over, evaluating them according to his purpose and finally choosing one, he took it from its place. Somehow, he managed to hide it on his person, where it stayed even after Hazel and her friend returned from the store. In fact, he downed some of the new liquor before going into the Craigs' bedroom, where he passed out on their bed. After sleeping for less than an hour, Sykes woke up. The party was still going strong in the other room.

Sykes and Hazel somehow managed to escape from the party under Sergeant Craig's view. Even with the rivers of alcohol at the house, Sykes and Hazel then went to the Blue Moon (a club in Fry), where they shared a few more drinks. It wasn't long before they left the Blue Moon and got back into the car. Sykes was driving. Just inside the gate to Fort Huachuca, Sykes turned off onto a dark, seemingly deserted road. Did he intend merely to "park" in a passable Lover's Lane? Or to plead his case by threatening Hazel? Whatever his plan, it didn't work. Instead, they argued. They argued bitterly, screaming, hitting, calling each other vile names. It didn't take long for Sykes to lose his temper. Drawing the finely-honed knife he had taken from the Craig kitchen, the enraged librarian struck out furiously, deeply slashing Hazel time and time again. He struck her in the chest, the neck, wherever he could find a place to drive in the sharp blade, continuing the attack even after his paramour was dead.

Then somehow, after it was over and still in somewhat of an alcoholic haze, he made his way back to the barracks where he cleaned himself up. Strangely, Sykes did not attempt to destroy the evidence; he simply stripped off his khaki uniform, soaked in blood, and left it tossed in the middle of the floor. Then, he crawled into his bunk and went to sleep.

At about 10:30 p.m., a roving guard found Hazel's badly mutilated body, soaked in blood. After identifying her, he went to the Craig home. Checking with her husband and remaining guests, the authorities learned Sykes had been at the party earlier. They found him still in the barracks, the knife laying beside his bloody clothes. The whole thing, from start (when Sykes arrived at the Craig house in Fry) to finish (when Hazel's body was found) took about two-and-a-half hours.

Sykes was arrested, tried in July of that same year, and convicted of murder. His sentence: hanging by the neck until dead. The sentence was carried out in January of the following year (1943) in a long, skinny, stone building originally intended as a warehouse called Building 31008.

Building 31008 is part of the post's earliest construction, pre-1900, when rock from Huachuca Creek was used to build the first permanent buildings. Visitors can see Building 31008 when they visit the historical section of Fort Huachuca called Old Post. Built into the hillside, it can appear at a certain angle to be single-story on one end, two stories on the other. It isn't, but it can look that way.

Building 31008 was originally built as a warehouse, but was the site of two hangings after sentencing for murder. (Courtesy of Ron Price.)

Legend, long since disproven, once had it that the building was deeper on one end to provide a "drop zone," a quick (and therefore more merciful) death when the trapdoor was sprung and a hooded body fell. A sign on the door still announces that it's the "Hangman's Warehouse."

Sykes was the second (and last) person to be executed by hanging on Fort Huachuca. Apparently, no one claimed the body. He was buried in the Post Cemetery "without honors," next to the one other man who earned the same fate. Both were later moved to an isolated corner of the cemetery. In an interesting twist of fate, the very location of their graves tends to generate curiosity. Visitors to the cemetery, looking about the peaceful site, are drawn to the isolated section where something is different. They walk about, looking for a clue, wondering why two graves are marked only with a name. So it shall be, for eons to come. Hazel Craig, the woman from Fry who could be said to have caused it all, is not buried on Fort Huachuca. She has been semi-forgotten.

In the meantime, it was still the early 1940s and the war affected everyone, on post or in town. There were telephones, even in downtown Fry, which generated long lines on payday as soldiers waited to call home. There was no television. Computers hadn't been invented. There was, however, radio. In addition to afternoon soap operas (so named because the commercials sold soap), groups of listeners gathered around the sets, eagerly devouring whatever snippet of news might be forthcoming.

At this time, rationing came into being. The way it worked was that a person or family would sign up, at which point they were issued a small booklet of stamps that allowed them to purchase rationed goods. The number of stamps authorized was calculated according to the number of people in the family. Without the ration stamps, no one could buy such things as nylons (stockings), sugar, bacon, butter, gasoline, tires, etc. With the stamps, one could often buy a limited amount of such items. Sometimes, extra "points" could be earned; for instance, one family picked cherries from their own trees and traded them for extra stamps. Mary O'Fallon remembers:

> It was my introduction to the insides of cherries; I was about 3 yrs old, and thought all cherries were red throughout. My mother and sister were picking the ripe ones, and gave me one to eat. I bit it in half, then looked at the half still in my hand. Next, I let out a blood-curdling screech and threw the remaining half away. I'd seen worms in apples and I thought the white "inside" of the cherry was another worm; and I thought that I'd eaten half of the worm!

Another thing that families did during rationing, according to Mary, was to render the fat out of bacon by cooking it, if you could get bacon. You actually saved the grease instead of throwing it away. You ate the bacon, of course. But

This image shows access to the Hangman's Warehouse, which is listed on the National Register of Historic Places. (Courtesy of Ron Price.)

the grease could be used to flavor a pot of beans or other foods, or it could be turned in for processing in exchange for more of other foods. "I think," Mary says, "it was used to make soap or something." Whatever it was used for, one thing is certain: people did collect grease and thereby earned additional points for their ration books.

Younger women of Fry, like those everywhere, were frustrated with the lack of nylon stockings, but they were quite resourceful in dealing with the situation. The most popular method was to go barelegged (popular now, especially in summer, but definitely not then). It wouldn't be acceptable if their legs were bare, though. To make it look as if they were wearing stockings, they would shave their legs and apply makeup to make them the color they would be if they were encased in stockings. However, stockings back then were seamed, so to complete the look, modern women used a mascara pencil to draw a line down the back of their legs. Dressed thus, many a lady would go grocery shopping at one of the two stores in town, the Fry Store (which by this time was leased to a Mrs. Stevens) and the Carmichael Store (operated by the Freihages). Similarly dressed, office workers—including those at Fort Huachuca—would go to work in faux nylons. They had to, because office women were not permitted to wear anything but skirts; no pants or slacks were allowed, and women's jeans weren't even invented yet.

UNITED STATES OF AMERICA
OFFICE OF PRICE ADMINISTRATION

(4) Nº 922177 CB

WAR RATION BOOK No. 3 — Void if altered

NOT VALID WITHOUT STAMP

Identification of person to whom issued: PRINT IN FULL

Katherine Z. Hollans
(First name) (Middle name) (Last name)

Street number or rural route

City or post office State

AGE	SEX	WEIGHT Lbs.	HEIGHT Ft. In.	OCCUPATION

SIGNATURE
(Person to whom book is issued. If such person is unable to sign because of age or incapacity, another may sign in his behalf.)

WARNING

This book is the property of the United States Government. It is unlawful to sell it to any other person, or to use it or permit anyone else to use it, except to obtain rationed goods in accordance with regulations of the Office of Price Administration. Any person who finds a lost War Ration Book must return it to the War Price and Rationing Board which issued it. Persons who violate rationing regulations are subject to $10,000 fine or imprisonment, or both.

OPA Form No. R-130

LOCAL BOARD ACTION

Issued by
(Local board number) (Date)

Street address

City State

(Signature of issuing officer)

This World War II Ration Book was issued to Katherine Hollans. (Courtesy of Kathy Mayo.)

The Mountain View Black Officers Club, begun because of military segregation, was built in 1942 at a cost of $78,000. Many big names appeared here duing World War II. Today, it is in serious disrepair and subject to destruction, although the Association of Buffalo Soldiers is attempting to have it restored and placed in the National Register of Historic Places. (Courtesy of Ron Price.)

In Fry's early days both before and after World War II, there was very little to do in the way of what would pass for popular entertainment. There were a few places like the Blue Moon where one could drink and dance; they weren't exactly considered "nice" and were frequented more by a rowdier contingent. The town wasn't very big, really more of a village. However, residents of Fry and surrounding communities often attended events on post as the guest of someone stationed at Fort Huachuca. There were actually two theaters-cum-nightclubs on Fort Huachuca where the troops, their families, and guests could attend the live shows.

One of the two clubs was and still is a very special building. Built in 1942 for just over $78,000, it was the 10,080-square-foot Mountain View Black Officer's Club. Before it was built, there was the Lakeside Club and later there would be the Hacienda Club, but in 1942, the troops were segregated. The fort had long been associated with the Buffalo Soldiers, the all-black 10th Cavalry; now, there were nearly 50,000 troops who trained at Fort Huachuca for the 92nd and 93rd Infantry Divisions, both of which were made up of black soldiers with white officers commanding. In a unique attempt to provide entertainment for everyone, Mountain View was built. The wooden building was of a kind then popular and part of what is often called "Splinter Village." It became historically important

Renamed especially for her appearance, the Lena Horne Theatre on Fort Huachuca is shown here in the 1940s. (Courtesy of the Fort Huachuca Historical Museum.)

because it was the only club in the United States that the army had ever built specifically for segregated troops. It would eventually be used as a general theater and for offices before deteriorating still further. (An attempt at restoration would be mounted in the future—more on that later.)

Mountain View was a great place to visit back then. Big stars appeared. Lena Horne appeared on stage at Fort Huachuca, her sultry voice giving a smoky tingle to many of the lonesome listeners. Dinah Shore was another star who came to Mountain View Black Officer's Club, where she sang and signed autographs; her cheerfully upbeat personality was a definite plus and very welcome. Even heavyweight boxing champ Joe Louis visited Fort Huachuca where, decked out in boxing gloves and satin robe, he helped dedicate a new recreation hall. When he did, those present responded with unparalleled enthusiasm, stomping feet, applauding loudly, howling in delight. Back then, big name stars were neither afraid nor too arrogant to appear at an isolated army post on the outskirts of a small village. It was wonderfully exciting!

Admittedly, Fry was small. The busiest intersection in town was where Garden Avenue crossed what would become Fry Boulevard. A few businesses clustered around the four corners and, because of the proximity of soldiers, most new ventures catered to the military. There was Keating's Service Station, a canteen, Carmichael's Store, a "club" (tavern), an adobe church, and more. During World War II, especially the latter years and immediately after, there was a lot of rapid business growth. The pulse of the town was definitely ambitious.

One popular business actually took place outside the town, but it subsequently affected town business. It was dude ranching. People with money, tourists, folks from "back East" and "up North" came from all over to visit Southern Arizona where they could sample life in the Wild West. They saw it in the movies, and now they could experience it for themselves. For the ranchers, it was a new way to make a living.

Other options developed for women. Previously, women were officially not permitted to enlist in the military, though it wasn't unknown for a woman to disguise herself as a man so she could join. Soldiering was thought to be for men. Women were expected to stay home, tending family and fields. During the war years, things changed. In big cities, women went to work in factories (Rosie the Riveter is synonymous with World War II), replacing men who had gone off to fight in the war. Women in these situations were found to be successful, so someone in Washington decided that if women were allowed to join the military, they could be assigned to support services. They could do office work, pack parachutes, ferry planes, or any number of things that would free up a fighting man.

Many women did decide to join the military services. Ruby Smith, one of 15 siblings, enlisted in the army; actually, her action was quite daring in the early

Dinah Shore signs autographs during her early 1940s appearance at Fort Huachuca. (Courtesy of the Fort Huachuca Historical Museum.)

1940s because many conservatives thought the military was for men and rowdier girls, not something "nice" girls would (or should) do. As one who wishes to remain discreet says, "My parents let me get married quite young because I told them it was either that—or I'd join the Army as soon as I was out of high school." In fact, in the early 1940s, women were not accepted as part of the Regular Army but were actually the Women's Auxiliary Army Corps (WAAC), which evolved into the Women's Army Corps. Of course, a portion of the Army became the Air Force, which allowed both men and women to become part of that service. So many of Ruby Smith's brothers and sisters would enlist (some in the navy, some in the army, some in the marines) that her stepmother Hazel Smith would, years later, receive a citation from General Nathan Twining for supplying so many Smiths to the armed forces. Ruby's nephew still lives in Sierra Vista.

At Fort Huachuca, the first female enlistee to arrive was Second Lieutenant Vera A. Harrison, reporting for duty on November 23, 1942. Not only was Harrison the first female soldier at Fort Huachuca, she was the first black member of the WAAC to serve with the men of the 93rd Infantry. Later that year, two companies of WAACs would be added to the roster at Fort Huachuca, but at the time she was

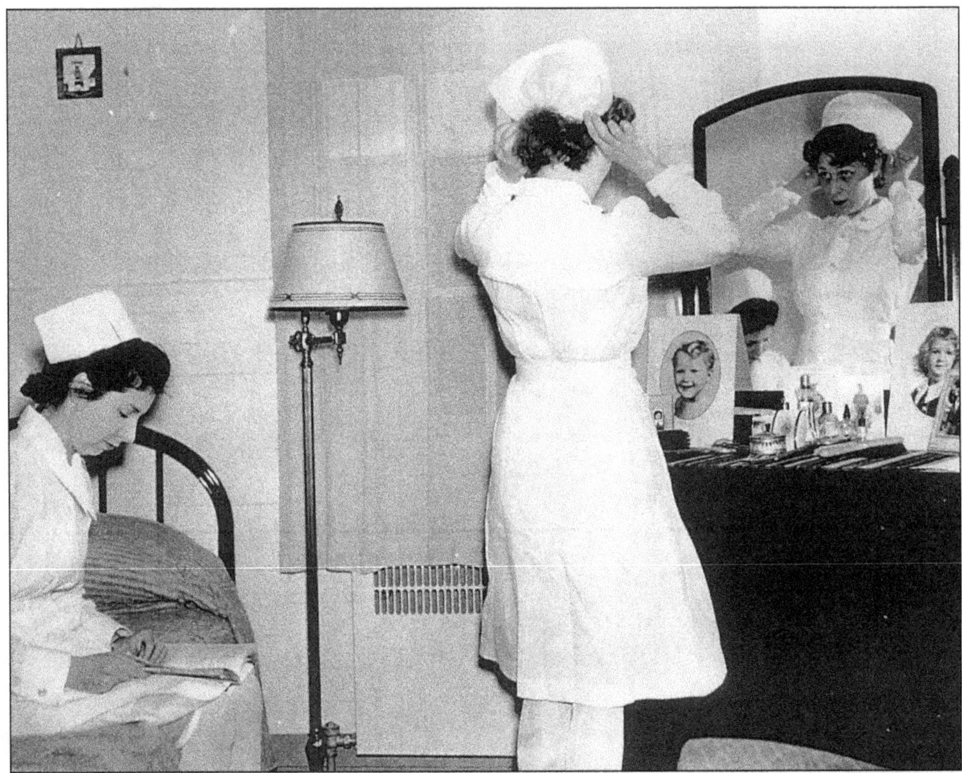

This image shows the inside of a World War II army nurse's quarters in 1942 at Fort Huachuca, as the young women prepare for work. (Courtesy of Fort Huachuca Historical Museum.)

Clara and Charles Wilson were mother and stepbrother to Nora Edmonson Walker, who would go on to be quite prominent in forming the new city of Sierra Vista. This picture was taken c. 1938. (Courtesy of Nola Edmonson Walker.)

assigned to a male unit. By the time the 32nd and 33rd Infantries were formed, the female soldiers would be housed in their own facilities.

Local resident Nola Edmondson chose to join the navy. Charles Wilson, Nola's father, was a union carpenter in Phoenix, but he moved from there to Hereford, where Nola was assigned to complete the inside of a homeowners residence, and from Hereford to Fort Huachuca. There, Nola worked for the post office until 1944. The family stayed in town until the war was over in 1945. Nola, exposed as she was to the army, chose to don the spiffy blue uniform of the navy. When asked why, Nola explains that her stepbrother Charles Wilson was in the navy and she so admired his rescue work and his heroism that when choosing a branch of the military to join, she chose the navy in his honor. It found her traveling to San Diego and New York. After her enlistment ended, she returned to Cochise County where she met and married Charles Walker. Charles was the eldest son of a respected ranching family. His parents were the owners of San Jose Ranch,

Nola Edmonson (now Walker) in uniform (1944) is shown after she joined the navy. Such enlisted women, for that branch of the military, were called WAVEs, or Women Accepted for Volunteer Emergency. (Courtesy of Nola Walker.)

which remains in the family to this day. Nola Walker would become quite active and somewhat notorious in helping form the local school district. Never a shy violet, she also played an extremely vital role in the incorporation and naming of Sierra Vista, where she still lives today. It's not the incorporation but the naming of the city that's always had a bit of truth hidden. It will be revealed herein.

In 1941, just a short time before Nola joined the navy, the Rural Electric Association (REA) brought electricity to Tombstone and a number of small towns in southeastern Arizona. People in big cities already had electricity, but not small villages, rural areas, or outlying ranches. The same year she joined the navy, electricity came to Benson, St. David, and Pomerene. By the early 1950s, even Elgin and Sonoita were included.

Not only did this advance mean an increase in agriculture because electric pumps were efficiently handling irrigation, but it wouldn't be long until kerosene lamps were put away for emergency use only. It meant refrigeration, so old-fashioned iceboxes were eventually phased out. It meant hot water on tap, without carrying it in and heating it on a big old kitchen range. And it meant radio in all the homes. Ralph Archer says:

> I remember hurrying home from school so I could get our chickens fed, eggs gathered, and homework done in time to listen to "The Cisco Kid" and "The Lone Ranger." On one, they advertised coffee and on the other one it was Butternut Bread. I can't remember which. Oh, and I liked "The Shadow." It seems like my sister listened to something called "Waltz Time" and "Your Hit Parade." I didn't pay much attention to those.

His sister, Janet, chimed in: "Oh, he's telling the truth about that!" she laughed.

> He was a typical boy. What he didn't say was while we were in school, our Mother would sometimes listen to soap operas. Most were only 15 minutes long, some were a half hour, and they were called that because their commercials were actually about soap. They must have thought women had nothing to be concerned about other than which brand of soap to buy. Heck, my grandma was still making her own lye soap!

Electric power was important to the people of Fry and to the whole operation at Fort Huachuca. It would help both communities grow, but it would also be important when things were downsized—as was about to happen.

9. Fort Huachuca's Deactivation and Reactivation

Somewhat unfortunately, development and growth in the Fry/Sierra Vista community hinged, and would continue to hinge, on how many soldiers were assigned to nearby Fort Huachuca. Some have dared to call Fry/Sierra Vista a "company town" and perhaps in many ways, it is. From the very beginning, the town existed to provide services and support to the army's nearby encampment. Naturally, when World War II ended, there was jubilation in the streets. Then reality hit: the end of fighting was the beginning of a downsized army. No longer needing the presence it once had, Fort Huachuca had no reason to continue heavy construction. The area lost many civilian workers and often their families as well; they had to go where the job took them and it wasn't here. Soldiers were no longer being assigned to Fort Huachuca, they weren't being trained there. Single or married, they either mustered out or got orders taking them elsewhere. The tiny town of Fry lost even more of its few customers.

It wasn't so much the soldiers themselves who made the changes difficult because there was actually very little social interaction between the soldiers and the townspeople. According to some, although a few things were shared, the symbiotic relationship of today did not exist. But because of the post, there were civilian employees who lived in town. When the soldiers went, so did many of them. Therefore, as small as Fry was, it didn't take long for the fort's downsizing to affect businesses. Several closed. It got even worse when, on September 15, 1947, Fort Huachuca was completely deactivated. Even the famed Apache Scouts were disbanded. (The Apache Scouts customarily enrolled for a period of from three months to a year, serving the military by tracking and helping locate their hostile, warring brothers. Because they knew the ways of their people and were "at home" in the southwest desert and nearby mountains, they were extremely effective. When all is said and done, they undoubtedly helped save many lives, although sometimes considered by their own people as traitorous. After the wars, the scouts began to deactivate. Some stayed on, serving at tasks like border control, fire lookouts, etc. Eventually, all that remained were relocated to Fort Huachuca, where they appeared in parades or reviews and in Hollywood movies. They stayed at Fort Huachuca until the last unit was disbanded in 1947.)

Not all was at an end for the Fry community, though. For some, the year 1947 was something of a beginning. That year, a cowboy named "Slim" Mayo left his employment at The Little Outfit, a ranch located west of Fort Huachuca. He had worked there for a number of years, conducting activities for visiting youngsters in addition to doing all the things a cowboy does, but Slim didn't ride off into the sunset. He simply saddled up his horse and rode east (into the sunrise?) to the fabled Y-Lightning Ranch belonging to the Mosons. He would stay there for many, many years, working the range and helping with the "Dudes and Dudettes," as he called them.

The tall, slender—from whence came his nickname—"cowboy's cowboy" set many a young lady's heart aflutter but, at the time of his relocation, he remained fancy free. All that was soon about to change. One day, he was in Patagonia, Arizona on business and happened to meet a spirited young woman who caught his fancy. Soon, he learned that she worked for the Southern Pacific Railroad, she was from Minnesota, and her name was Katherine Holluns (called "Kay"). The cowboy was definitely smitten! Turning on all his charm, he courted Kay, and in November 1947, she became Mrs. Kay Mayo. The following September saw the

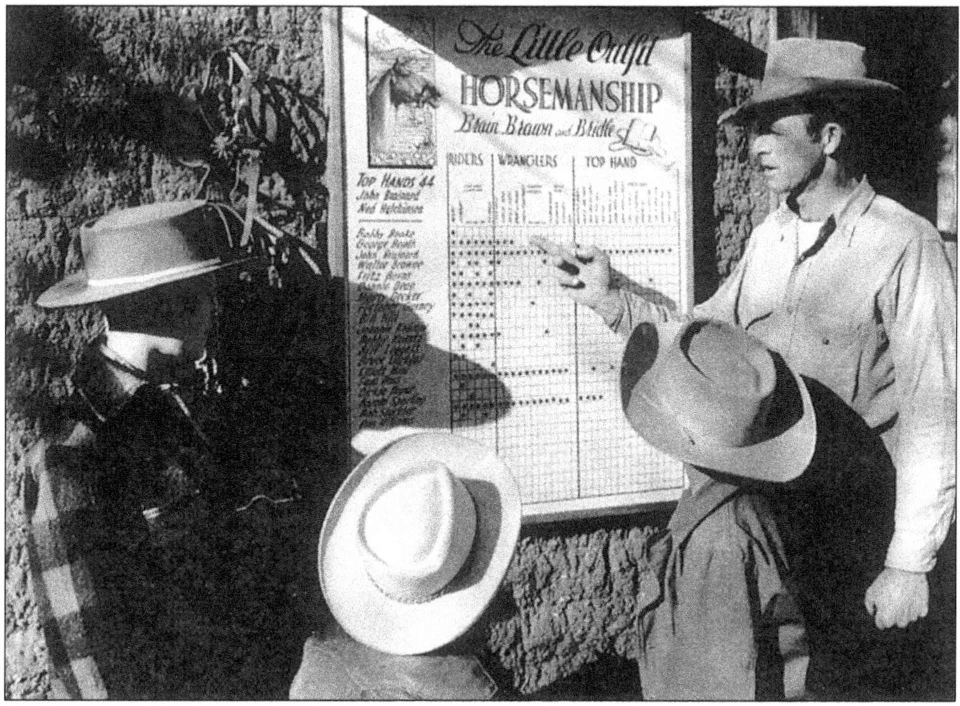

Slim Mayo is shown here displaying a score chart to young buckaroos at the Little Outfit. (Courtesy of Kathy Mayo.)

birth of Slim and Kay's only daughter, Kathy. (Kay and Kathy still live in Sierra Vista today.)

So, the times weren't all gloomy; there were bright spots of happiness and anticipation. However, there was still the general downsizing to contend with. The local school, which in 1939 enrolled 35 students, had grown to 450 at the beginning of World War II. However, after the war, it dropped back to the original number. There were not enough students to fill classrooms, so many of the teachers had to be let go, which caused a ripple effect in the town. Losing a paycheck meant leaving the community, which often led to an even smaller enrollment. Yet to pay the bills and feed their own families, they had to go teach somewhere else. So around and around it went.

As the downturn continued and people lost their homes or businesses, some residents who could afford it gambled on the future by buying up a substantial

Slim Mayo and his bride Katherine (Kay), on their wedding day, are standing outside the Canelo store, which no longer exists. (Courtesy of Kay Mayo.)

number of residential and commercial properties for pennies on the dollar. Reportedly, Erwin Fry was one citizen who could (and did) do such a thing. Many sellers were desperate, they simply wanted to cut their losses and get out of the market, if they were lucky, with a little traveling money to take them on to a new location and a new job. For some, it would be too late; properties were foreclosed and their owners lost everything. Many a hard-working father was humbled, helpless to do more than pack and take their families elsewhere. It didn't matter that tears rolled down the faces of kids leaving perhaps the only home they had ever known, leaving behind their friends and maybe their beloved pets. Many a mother clutched a young child close, comforting them, whispering that some other place would be even better.

In many ways, since Fry was a rural community, it survived somewhat better than it might have otherwise. If families had a cow, there was milk and butter. People raised chickens for the meat and eggs. One woman says, "I never got so damned tired of fried chicken in my whole life! Every day it was chicken, chicken, chicken! Or beans—you wouldn't believe how many kinds of beans there are. We had beans almost every night. Beans and fried chicken." Many folks raised produce in their own gardens, and several had fruit trees. Some of the older residents made their own lye soap. It all helped but still, times were rough. Very rough. Some have compared those days to the Great Depression and, while it was quite different in most ways, there were a few similarities.

One little-known side effect of the Fort Huachuca downsizing and deactivation is that many of the army families—like the terminated workers in town—had pets they couldn't (or wouldn't) take with them. Sadly, without any true local government, there was no such thing as an animal control shelter and no way to quickly find homes for the number of pets that existed. Many were simply turned loose, left to fend for themselves, to hunt whatever they could find to eat, and to multiply exponentially.

Most were abandoned in what is now the residential portion of the post, and they probably hung around for a little while, waiting forlornly for their owners to return. When that didn't happen, hunger forced the animals to widen their territory. It wasn't long before they ranged throughout the less-inhabited areas near the county's western border and into Canelo. There are two things about dogs: they are usually social creatures, and they're smart. Therefore, it's not surprising that they soon formed new "families," running in packs much like their wild ancestors. The dogs had figured out that a pack, working together with a good leader, can bring down more game. Unfortunately, before long they graduated from hunting rabbits, deer, and other wild game to attacking cattle. That meant area ranchers faced some real problems. Cattle were their livelihood, the way they paid their bills and fed their families, and suddenly that livelihood was being destroyed by dangerously hungry animals.

There simply were not enough people left to take in that many pets, even had they wanted to do so. In addition, there was another problem: could the animals, after fighting for survival, after learning to kill for food, ever have been returned

Nearby is the small community called Canelo, a word that in Spanish means "cinnamon" and refers to the color of the mountainside in the dry season. (Courtesy of Ron Price.)

to civilization, to domestication? It's debatable and, at this point, moot. What did happen is that ranchers began defending their property. Because they lived where one might encounter wolves, bears, bobcats, and poisonous snakes at almost any time, the ranchers and cowboys all carried weapons. According to one informant, they began shooting the wild dogs, eliminating them and disposing of the carcasses in large pits.

It has been suggested that the large open space north of today's Highway 90 Bypass, east of Highway 90, is where one such large pit was dug and many carcasses buried. Perhaps, according to one urban legend, that is where the name "Graveyard Gulch" came from; after all, when some excavation was done, bones were found nearby. Were they animal bones or human? There is no cemetery out there, according to the informant, who was born, grew up, and returned to Sierra Vista for health reasons after relocating for a few years—and who asks to remain unidentified. If the bones were human, he says it was probably someone buried in an unmarked grave as a wagon train passed through 100 years earlier.

A related theory is that the bones, if human, were the result of some long-ago Indian attack. The entire area was so isolated during the Apache Wars that no cemetery would have existed and, with a simple burial, no record made. Similarly, whether killed in an attack or not, individuals were often buried with a simple wooden marker that would have disintegrated over time. The third theory is, of course, that the carcasses of animals destroyed during the hard times while Fort Huachuca was deactivated were buried here. There may be a record somewhere of an investigation and determination about the bones. Regardless, like most urban legends, the theories continue with each one embroidered more than the last.

The good news? The hard times would not last. The bad news? It was because of the Korean War that Fort Huachuca was reactivated and conditions in Fry improved.

Reactivation of the fort took place on April 20, 1951. Suddenly, new troops were pouring into Fort Huachuca and in the little village outside its gates, and things were buzzing. Pay phones were back on the post, along with a few more in town.

In 1949, local telephone service had started with lines coming from the post and Fry, but its exchange was 23 miles away in the thriving copper-mining town of Bisbee, the county seat. Fry was too small. The exchange had suffered during the earlier downsizing and deactivation. During the rough times, equipment was packed up and moved north to Eloy, a small village located south of Phoenix, of

The fort entrance is shown here in 1951, during a downsizing just before Fort Huachuca was reactivated. This is the desolate North Gate, closest to Campstone, which is now Huachuca City. (Courtesy of Fort Huachuca Historical Museum.)

all places. Why Eloy? Who knows? But it wouldn't be the phone service's final stop. With reactivation of Fort Huachuca in 1951, the United States needed phone service on post so the equipment was moved back to the fort. Then when the Korean Conflict was over, the post was deactivated once again, and with that action, the phone service moved all its equipment from the post again. This time, they took it to San Manuel, a mining town on the other side of the mountains north of Tucson.

In 1953, it would return and Fry would have its first phonebook. Actually, it wasn't quite a book; it was printed on a card, maybe 4 inches by 6 inches. At the top was a rectangle with the telephone company's logo between the words "Telephone Directory" and, centered right underneath, it said "FRY" (no state mentioned); just under that and also centered was "Fall 1953." The numbers were all simple four-digit numbers with no prefix. In what could perhaps be

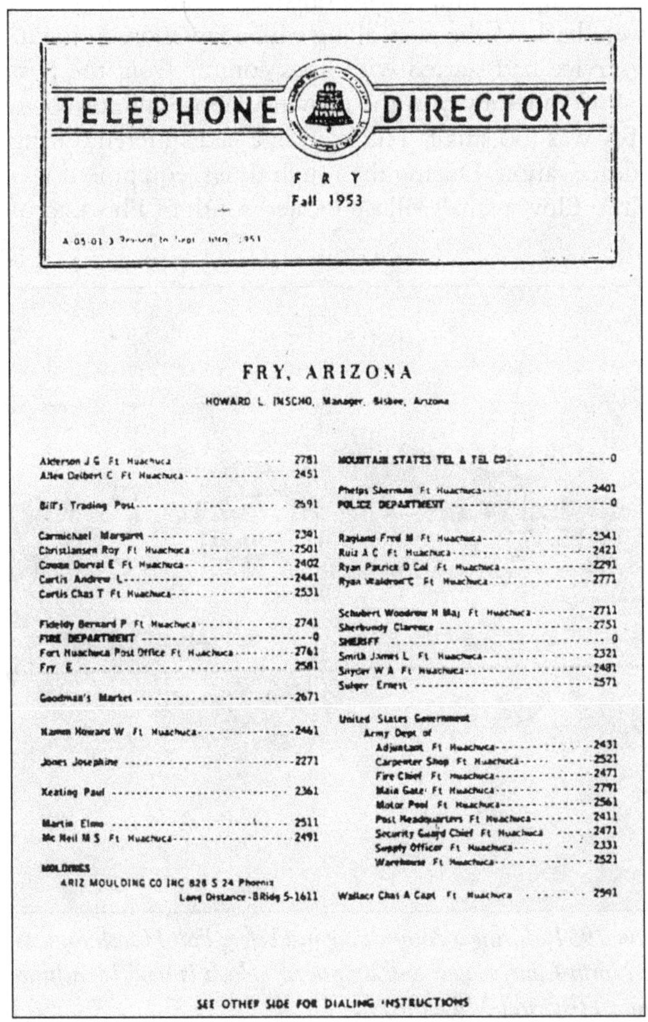

TELEPHONE DIRECTORY

F R Y

Fall 1953

FRY, ARIZONA

HOWARD L. INSCHO, Manager, Bisbee, Arizona

Alderson J G Ft Huachuca ---- 2781
Allen Delbert C Ft Huachuca ---- 2451

Bill's Trading Post ---- 2591

Carmichael Margaret ---- 2391
Christiansen Roy Ft Huachuca ---- 2501
Cowan Dorval E Ft Huachuca ---- 2402
Curtis Andrew L ---- 2441
Curtis Chas T Ft Huachuca ---- 2531

Fideldy Bernard P Ft Huachuca ---- 2741
FIRE DEPARTMENT ---- 0
Fort Huachuca Post Office Ft Huachuca ---- 2761
Fry E ---- 2581

Goodman's Market ---- 2671

Hamm Howard W Ft Huachuca ---- 2461

Jones Josephine ---- 2271

Keating Paul ---- 2361

Martin Elmo ---- 2511
Mc Neil M S Ft Huachuca ---- 2491

MOULDINGS
ARIZ MOULDING CO INC 828 S 24 Phoenix
Long Distance-BRidg 5-1611

MOUNTAIN STATES TEL & TEL CO ---- 0

Phelps Sherman Ft Huachuca ---- 2401
POLICE DEPARTMENT ---- 0

Ragland Fred M Ft Huachuca ---- 2341
Ruiz A C Ft Huachuca ---- 2421
Ryan Patrick D Col Ft Huachuca ---- 2291
Ryan Waldron C Ft Huachuca ---- 2771

Schubert Woodrow H Maj Ft Huachuca ---- 2711
Sherbundy Clarence ---- 2751
SHERIFF ---- 0
Smith James L Ft Huachuca ---- 2321
Snyder W A Ft Huachuca ---- 2481
Sulger Ernest ---- 2571

United States Government
Army Dept of
Adjutant Ft Huachuca ---- 2431
Carpenter Shop Ft Huachuca ---- 2521
Fire Chief Ft Huachuca ---- 2471
Main Gate Ft Huachuca ---- 2791
Motor Pool Ft Huachuca ---- 2561
Post Headquarters Ft Huachuca ---- 2411
Security Guard Chief Ft Huachuca ---- 2471
Supply Officer Ft Huachuca ---- 2331
Warehouse Ft Huachuca ---- 2521

Wallace Chas A Capt Ft Huachuca ---- 2591

SEE OTHER SIDE FOR DIALING INSTRUCTIONS

Dated 1953, this publication is the entire telephone directory—the first one ever—for Fry. (Courtesy of Henry Hauser Museum.)

This state-of-the-art commissary at Fort Huachuca is shown during the 1950s. There were only two small stores in Sierra Vista and most everyone on the post got their groceries here. (Courtesy of the Fort Huachuca Historical Museum.)

called the first yellow pages (though actually part of the general directory), there was one service listing (for the Fort Huachuca Post Office) and three businesses: Bill's Trading Post, Goodman's Market, and a single out-of-town (long distance) listing for Arizona Moulding Company, Inc., in Phoenix. There was a series of nine numbers for the United States government Department of the Army (Fort Huachuca). To reach the Mountain States Telephone & Telegraph Company, the police, fire, or sheriff's departments, one simply dialed "0" and the operator would connect you forthwith. There was no listing for an electric company, although the REA existed and service was provided, and no listing for a water company. The 1953 Fry directory did list 25 individuals, 17 of them on Fort Huachuca. This means there were eight private telephones in Fry; at that time, one did not own a phone—it was rented. Alphabetically, the names of Fry residents in that first directory were: Margaret Carmichael; Andrew Curtis; E. (Erwin) Fry; Josephine Jones; Paul Keating; Elmo Martin; Clarence Sherbundy; and Ernest Sulger.

About the same time, another rather enterprising individual set up a unique form of an old business. As Marie Storment tells it, Madam (no one remembers—or will admit to remembering—her name) owned a beautiful old LaSalle touring car with heavy curtains on the windows. That car served as her place of business, but she wasn't conducting sightseeing trips! What she would do is take one of

Keating's Service Station, with owner Paul Keating, is shown here in 1950 and was located just outside the Main Gate of Fort Huachuca. It is where Madam would fill the tank of her old LaSalle touring car that she used for "business," especially on army paydays. (Courtesy of the Henry Hauser Museum.)

the "girls" who worked for her for a ride in the backseat. Madam did the driving. Madam would go up to the main gate of Fort Huachuca, pick up a soldier customer, and drive the couple straight down the busy main drag (today's Fry Boulevard). Remember, the touring car had heavy curtains, which prevented citizens from seeing activity inside the LaSalle. The LaSalle purred all the way past the edge of town (it didn't take long in such a small town) and on to the San Pedro River. There, she would turn the car around and go back to the starting point. By that time, business had been conducted, so the current passenger would exit the vehicle and a new one was picked up. From that point, it was the same story over again, the same round-trip. Over and over again, business was conducted all day and into the night. Of course, those who recognized the car also knew what was going on and snickered behind their hands.

The LaSalle would be called a gas-guzzler today, but in the early 1950s, gasoline was relatively cheap. At the same time, the car was large, comfortable, and gave quite a smooth ride—not that the car's passengers really paid much attention to luxury or comfort. Keating's gas station was close to the main gate of Fort Huachuca, a fortunate state of affairs for Madam. Army paydays were definitely her busiest times and she used more gasoline than usual, because of the round-trips from the main gate to the San Pedro River.

Once asked about her portable brothel, Madam replied "Why not? It saves having to pay rent somewhere, and controls the time used for each transaction." The red light district had definitely gone mobile!

During the same years as this colorful bit of Fry/Sierra Vista's history, there were some forward-thinking people angling for the community's own school district. So far, there had been elementary schools somewhat nearby (i.e., Buena School) but none in Fry, and definitely no high school. Fry/Sierra Vista had its own grade school district but at the same time was assigned to the Tombstone Union School District. That meant all high school students were bused to Tombstone, where district headquarters were located. Tombstone liked it that way, even though they needed 16 buses, running twice a day, every day. One official there was overheard to say that not having the Fry students attend school in Tombstone meant a substantial loss in revenues, and one gentleman—Pete Keller, a deputy sheriff and school board member—said flat-out, "You'll get a school district over my dead body!"

However, a group of local citizens could see future growth, understood the need for a local school district, and wanted a local high school. And, on February 1, 1954, Fort Huachuca was (once more, for the last time to date) reactivated. Its commander would get involved in the local school situation, a problem whose denouement took place about the same time as the city's battle for incorporation.

Until Sierra Vista got their own high school, students entering the upper levels had to attend classes in Tombstone. Eventually, it would lead to a confrontation and the creation of a new high school district. In the meantime, the 1932 graduating class at Tombstone, shown here, celebrated graduation with the customary picnic. There were 12 students in the class, including Jim Rice and June Fry. (Courtesy of the Henry Hauser Museum.)

The idea of incorporating had been tossed around for quite a while but the real furor actually began in 1955 when a group of local citizens first petitioned for incorporation and a name change from Fry to something else. On August 8, 1955, nominations were taken for an interim city council, should the petition for incorporation be accepted; they were William Daniels, Mrs. Gilbert Daniels, a Mrs. Delaney, Rose Ferrell, Frank Freihage, Nellie Freihage, Clara Getzwiller, Paul Keating, Elmo Martin, Paul Nott, Harold Parks, Pat Parks, Bill Peterson, Joe Vogler, a Mr. Wales, Nola (Mrs. Charles) Walker, and Paul Wolfe. Not all would be appointed, but these were the initial names entered into nomination.

The petition to incorporate and have the town's name changed was signed by more than two-thirds of the taxpayers and filed with the county Board of Supervisors on August 15, 1955, just one week following the meeting to nominate a city council. The petition for incorporation was declined and the real fight began. Accusations of illegality would be filed and defended, threats of violence uttered, and Erwin Fry's pride and stubbornness concerning the matter—though he was certainly within his legal rights—would end not in preventing incorporation, but only in making it more expensive. Furthermore, though he was well within his legal rights in managing his property, his actions condemned a small portion of the overall community to a long-term lack of city services.

This rare photo shows Erwin Fry, the man for whom Fry Boulevard is named, and Lillian Rice Fry as they visit Tuscon. (Courtesy of the Henry Hauser Museum.)

10. Incorporating and Naming Sierra Vista

In the mid-1950s, what was the community missing? According to some, it was a newspaper. Residents had for years been forced to rely on news as reported (and slanted) in the Tombstone and Bisbee papers. There wasn't one specifically for the local area, not one that reported news and events important to the people who lived here. The nearest they'd ever come was more than three decades earlier (in May 1920) when there was a mimeographed news sheet called the *Buffalo Bulletin* published on Fort Huachuca. It quickly grew from 5 to 12 pages, from a circulation of 100 copies to nearly 1,500. Regulations were its downfall. Unfortunately, it was published by soldiers who, though they recognized the need for a paper, didn't have government approval. Adding to the problem, they published the *Bulletin* on government property, using government equipment and supplies. It was a classic catch-22 situation. Everyone agreed that paper, ink, etc. cost money, but the U.S. Army would neither subsidize publication nor permit the acceptance of paid advertising. In fact, because publication was done on government property using government supplies and equipment, the enterprising soldiers couldn't even sell subscriptions. The frustrated soldier-publishers struggled for about a year and a half, hanging on by the skin of their teeth, trying to get the army's approval. It wasn't granted. Finally, the *Bulletin* folded and readers of this community were forced to make do with out-of-town papers.

There wouldn't be a "local" paper until the *Huachuca Herald*, named for Fort Huachuca, made its first appearance on October 7, 1955. The summer of that year, Lois and H.H. "Ky" Richards moved to the unincorporated community. Lois claimed to have flunked English in college, but supported her husband's desire to put out a paper. They began with a tabloid-size publication, doing all the work themselves. At the time, the *Herald* was taking quite a chance locating in Fry/Sierra Vista; though the name *Huachuca Herald* seems to indicate it could have been published in either Fry/Sierra Vista or Huachuca City, it's important to recall that the paper was not named for either community. Any knowledgeable businessman looking to the future would want to establish roots and be associated with the more successful locale. Each of the two communities was located just outside one of Fort Huachuca's gates, and each was sure they'd be the most prosperous. What caused Richards to choose the Fry/Sierra Vista area? Maybe it was personally intuitive foresight and a gut feeling. After all, most experts were predicting that Huachuca City (to the north) would grow and be bigger than Fry. (Most publications say "bigger than Sierra Vista," but the truth is that Sierra Vista didn't exist until later. At this point, the town was still called Fry and, on down the bumpy road going east, Buena. The experts' assumption may have been justified if the early predictions refer only to Fry. But if they were talking about the future Sierra Vista, we now know they were misguided.) The new *Huachuca Herald* started as a weekly but soon grew to a twice weekly publication. This forward-thinking and enterprising newspaper would detail the difficult birth of a new town that would be named Sierra Vista.

Erwin Fry and his wife Lillian Rice Fry are shown here in Phoenix. They were not easy to capture on film. (Courtesy of the Henry Hauser Museum.)

The biggest stumbling block to incorporating the town was Erwin Fry, who had been invited to join the pro-incorporation group and declined. He and a band of other property owners wanted to keep the town as it was—a little village named Fry, where he was in control. There seems to be some indication the name would not be retained after incorporation. After all, he was one of the earliest residents, having come to the area as a teenager. He was the one who married the teacher, Lillian Rice, and together they created Fry by building a store (with post office) and placing their name on the building. When the name was accepted as the community name, Erwin Fry was a big deal and he didn't want that taken away from him. But as a current resident wryly says, "Well, he owned the land. He could do what he wanted to do."

Yes, and what he wanted to do was retain his namesake town as is. He would fight tooth and nail to keep the status quo; the name was not only his family's legacy but his personal identity. Rumor has it that he would have given in and permitted incorporation if the name Fry would be retained, but that idea fizzled.

Round one came shortly after the first incorporation attempt. As reported in the *Huachuca Herald* on October 28, 1955, Erwin Fry and his wife had filed papers just over two months earlier, claiming the incorporation was not legal because there were not enough signatures on the petitions. There were 189 signatures, but Fry (through his attorney) claimed 200 or more were necessary. It didn't matter that the county board of supervisors approved both the petition and the formation of a five-member city council. Its prospective members were suggested, including Rudy Steffen as mayor. Erwin Fry would have none of it; the rivalry and infighting would grow bitter.

On November 18, 1955, the *Herald*—which still contained ads calling the community both Fry and Sierra Vista—reported that Sierra Vista had probably lost around $10,000 in tax revenues by not being in a position to take its share of state refunds. To be eligible, Mayor Rudy Steffen explained, a new municipality must have a recognized population census. The Arizona Tax Commission was willing and eager to award the fledgling town its fair share of monies collected, just as soon as the census count was made. In a catch-22 situation, the council then pointed out there could be no population count by a team from the Bureau of the Census as long as there was any cloud over the incorporation.

Put simply, that meant that by suing over the number of signatures on the petition and declaring the first incorporation illegal, Erwin Fry and his wife created the clouds hanging over incorporation. They quite effectively prevented the refund of substantial tax revenues that could have been used to improve services (such as adequate health, police and fire protection, street work, etc.) in and around the community.

At the same time, bad news arrived from the Federal Housing Authority (FHA). Housing was in short supply since the post reactivated, and there had recently been a proposal to build around 50 rental units to help the situation. When the announcement was made of their anticipated construction, George Hilliar (then

Another well-known Arizonian, Senator Barry Goldwater, visited the troops at Fort Huachuca. He was met at LAAF by Brigadier General Gerd Grumbacher, shown here as he walks alongside Goldwater. (Courtesy of the Fort Huachuca Historical Museum.)

head of the FHA in Arizona) unequivocally stated that he did not believe in rental housing outside the metropolitan areas of Phoenix and Tucson.

FHA excuses for not going ahead with the project here and in Tombstone indicated it wasn't their fault, that contractors messed up and didn't meet alleged deadlines. An editorial of the time posited that the FHA made no effort to notify the respective communities that the project would die unless certain conditions were met prior to specific deadlines. There was a cloak of secrecy surrounding the project from the very beginning, it was said, from when bids were solicited and received (in May) until information leaked out that there would be no rentals for Sierra Vista. The implication is that the sister project in Tombstone was also dead.

In the meantime, George Hilliar (who was an appointee of Senator Barry Goldwater) was "promoted" to a Washington job. And announcements were made that the army promised Fort Huachuca a total of more than 1,100 housing units on post. People in nearby Sierra Vista/Fry called the whole rental housing episode a veritable "fiasco," and said they had been misled into spending time and money on a project when there was no intention of cooperation from the FHA.

Still, the city council didn't give up on dreams of incorporation, but it had given up much of its county support services. Everything Cochise County had done previously was now the responsibility of the fledgling city. Unfortunately,

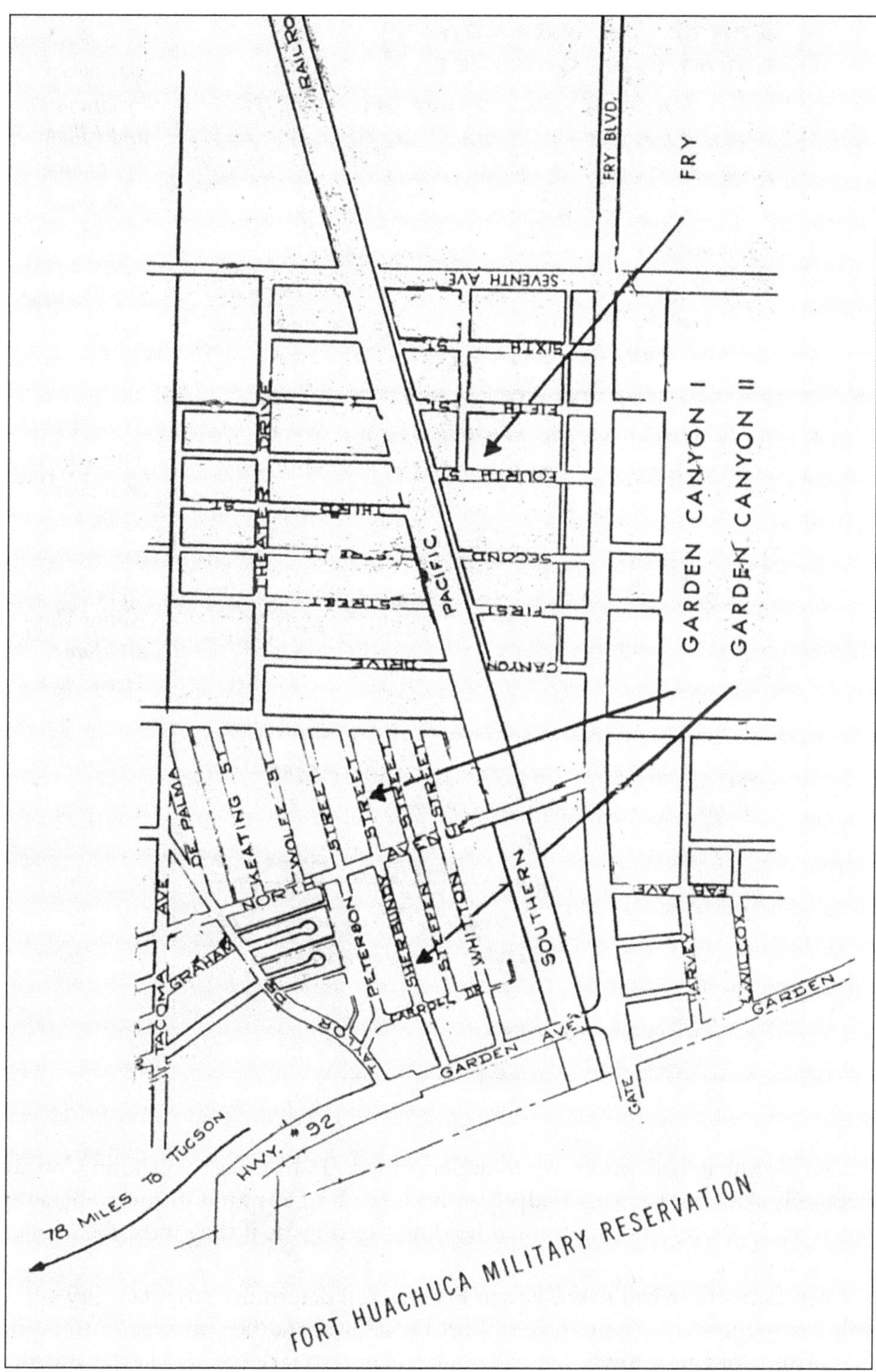

This street map shows Garden Canyon and Fry, or the early Sierra Vista area. The railroad, which no longer exists, cut right through the city. (Courtesy of Rosario Guzman.

STATE OF ARIZONA } ss
COUNTY OF COCHISE }

KNOW ALL MEN BY THESE PRESENTS:– THAT WE, ERWIN FRY AND LILLIAN S. FRY, HIS WIFE, DO HEREBY CERTIFY THAT WE HAVE CAUSED THE ACCOMPANYING PLAT TO BE MADE BY RALPH L. MOTZ, REGISTERED ENGINEER; AND WE DO HEREBY DEDICATE TO THE USE OF THE PUBLIC FOREVER THOSE STREETS, DRIVES AND ALLEYS SHOWN THEREON.

IN WITNESS WHEREOF, WE HAVE HEREUNTO SET OUR HANDS THIS 2ND DAY OF JULY, 1955.

Erwin Fry
ERWIN FRY

Lillian S. Fry
LILLIAN S. FRY

STREET

Subscribed and sworn to before me, a Notary Public, by the persons whose names are subscribed above, this 2nd day of July, 1955

[signature]
Notary Public, in and for the County of Cochise, Arizona

My commission expires 10-25-55

SECOND

This document was signed by Erwin and Lillian Fry to build additions to Fry. He would refuse to have Fry Townsite included in the later-to-be incorporated Sierra Vista. This original document is on file in the city offices. (Courtesy of Kathy Mayo and James Herrewig.)

the city council had never been underwritten. It had been operating on an extremely skinny shoestring budget, without funds of any kind to cover operating expenses. However, they continued holding meetings as if they were the council for a real town.

Then came more bad news. Erwin Fry was still determined to retain Fry as the only town outside the main gate of Fort Huachuca, and he continued protesting the forming of a new town. He had gone so far as to take his case to the attorney general's office, where it was decided that the courts would handle the matter if the two sides didn't settle in the meantime. Realizing that license fees would bring some money into town coffers, the council drafted and prepared to act on a new ordinance involving the issuance of licenses for new community businesses. Suddenly, Dan Moore (the city attorney) advised the council to halt proceedings until the incorporation matter was settled. Until it was settled, the town simply didn't exist. The *Huachuca Herald* reported on Friday, December 2, 1955, that the city council had been stopped in its tracks because there were clouds over legality of the city's incorporation. It wasn't entirely true; the council was merely regrouping.

Unfortunately, Moore's declaration meant the council could not pass any ordinance that would produce revenues to cover operating expenses. Frustrated councilmen admitted being stymied, but asserted that it was only temporary. In the meantime, it was doubted that even residential development could take place until the incorporation was declared legal. Still, the council didn't give up.

Furthermore, on December 8, Mayor Rudy Steffen said the incorporation issue was not dead and the complaint filed three days earlier was the beginning of a court action originating from Erwin Fry's opposition. But, Steffen said, the action could have an unexpected effect; it could give the Superior Court the impetus it needed to decide whether the city was legal or not.

It definitely seemed as if people in Sierra Vista wanted incorporation. A group called the Garden Canyon Pioneers came out strongly in favor of the incorporation, and said they were going to support the appointed council. Others were strongly against the way the matter was handled in the *Bisbee Daily Review* (Bisbee was, and is, the county seat). Representing the signers of the original petition, city councilmen asserted that incorporation news, as reported in the Bisbee paper, was "slanted" in favor of the Frys. A comprehensive letter of protest, dated December 7, was sent to Robert Page (president of Phelps-Dodge, which held a controlling interest in the *Daily Review*).

In the same issue (December 8) of the *Herald*, it was reported that Attorney General Robert Morrison asked, in a complaint filed in Cochise County's Superior Court, that the incorporation be declared illegal. It gets interesting because the document was filed by James McNulty, who represented the Frys but was also acting as special agent for the attorney general. Some called it a conflict of interest and were downright angry at McNulty's involvement. Morrison figuratively threw down the gauntlet, challenging the right of Sierra Vista's Mayor Steffen and the pre-incorporation council members to hold office. Remember: the incorporation, though accepted by most locals, was not official and had not been accepted by the State of Arizona. So far as the state was concerned, the Town of Sierra Vista (soon to be the City of Sierra Vista) didn't exist; at least, not officially. How could there be a mayor and city council holding office if the city didn't exist? The complaint had each council member subject to $2,000 in fines for a total of $10,000, definitely big money in 1955.

In rebuttal, council members circulated their claim that a local government should provide the basic needs of any growing community. They pointed out the great need for locally improved sanitation, for police and fire protection, for recreational facilities, better streets and street lighting. In addition, the council pointed out, incorporation was a forerunner to drawing up zoning regulations that would prevent haphazard and random development. It would, they said, contribute to the orderly planned growth of Sierra Vista. "The people of Sierra Vista," said Mayor Steffen, "want incorporation and we're going to fight any attempt to take it away."

In the meantime, residents were questioning why Attorney General Morrison was involving himself in a matter which should have been settled between Erwin Fry and the people of Sierra Vista. They believed the attorney general was taking sides with one particular property owner against the majority, and they wondered why. They were not quiet with their questions and conclusions. The swell of public opinion grew, the grumbling getting louder.

Less than two weeks after Morrison issued his first opinion on the matter, he retracted it. Charging that he was being made a scapegoat in the matter, Morrison quickly stopped the suit he had filed in Bisbee at the Cochise County Superior Court. His letter to Mayor Steffen became a matter of public record. In it, he addresses the town as both Sierra Vista and Fry but acknowledges Steffen as mayor. Its text is as follows:

> December 10, 1955
> Honorable R.W. Steffen, Mayor
> City of Sierra Vista
> Fry, Arizona
>
> Dear Mayor:
> I was shocked at the interpretation, inferences and innuendoes that have arisen as a result of the complaint that was authorized by me to be filed which challenges the legality of the incorporation of Sierra Vista. I have read the stories in the *Bisbee Daily Review* and the December 9th copy of the *Huachuca Herald*. One thing is apparent from the newspaper stories and that is that the people of Cochise County and, in particular, Sierra Vista were never informed that preliminary discussions and consultations were had with persons purportedly representing Sierra Vista and the objectors to incorporation. The action I filed was the result of these discussions and was intended to be a friendly suit agreed to by all concerned. However, I would say from what I have read that the suit has developed to be anything but friendly.
>
> I was left under the impression that you and the council understood clearly that the only purpose behind the lawsuit was to legally determine the legality of the incorporation so that when your city made claims for sales tax revenue from the State Treasurer, the question of legality of the incorporation of Sierra Vista could not be raised and sales tax revenue would be paid to Sierra Vista. Otherwise, Sierra Vista might have to expend sums of money for a census to no avail if its incorporation

CLASS OF SERVICE
This is a full-rate Telegram or Cablegram unless its deferred character is indicated by a suitable symbol above or preceding the address.

WESTERN UNION (34)

A. N. WILLIAMS, PRESIDENT — NEWCOMB CARLTON, CHAIRMAN OF THE BOARD — J. C. WILLEVER, FIRST VICE-PRESIDENT

SYMBOLS
DL=Day Letter
NT=Overnight Telegram
LC=Deferred Cable
NLT=Cable Night Letter
Ship Radiogram

The filing time shown in the date line on telegrams and day letters is STANDARD TIME at point of origin. Time of receipt is STANDARD TIME at point of destination

CA192 52/50 DL 5 EXTRA=EMPORIA VIR 23 451P

MISS KATHERINE HOLLUNS=

GRANDMAROIS MINN=

CAN OFFER YOU PERMANENT STENOGRAPHER POSITION AT $19.00 A WEEK AT JOHNS MANVILLE JARRATT WITH INCREASE IN SIX MONTH IF DESERVING. PRESENT MAXIMUM RATE OF JOB IS $25.00 WIRE COLLECT TO ADDRESS BELOW IF INTERESTED AND CAN REPORT FOR WORK BY SEPTEMBER SEVENTH OR SOONER=

H L PIERSON 406 TILLAR ST EMPORIA VA.

$19.00 $25.00 406.

This telegram caused Katherine Holluns to leave her family home in Minnesota. She'd eventually work in Patagonia, then marry Slim Mayo. (Courtesy of Kay Mayo.)

> should be declared invalid in a test suit to determine the propriety of the State Treasurer to pay sales tax revenue to it.
>
> I was under the impression that all this was commonly known and understood and that the lawsuit that I authorized to be filed would be a friendly one for the sole purpose of removing the cloud that has hung over Sierra Vista since its incorporation.
>
> Personally, I would do anything within my power to help perfect a city in your community and I had no thought to do anything to prevent such an eventuality. It is my opinion that the opponents of incorporation are concerned only with their own personal welfare.

Thus, the state's attorney general did put an end to the question and did declare that the people of Sierra Vista and its appointed city council could go ahead with incorporation proceedings.

Charlie Elledge, the man who witnessed and told about the Naco Incident, had moved first to Huachuca City, then to Sierra Vista when it was still Fry. He and Erwin worked together on several home-building projects and, as a result, became good friends. Before he died, Charlie said that if the first city council had been nice to Erwin Fry, there wouldn't have been any trouble. Fry was, according to Charlie, actually in favor of incorporation at one time, but the city manager of the new town made the mistake of saying to Charlie, "We're going to shove incorporation down Erwin Fry's and your throat!"

Charlie didn't back down. He told the man that if it was what they wanted, all they had to do was buy the land. He and Erwin would pack up everything in a suitcase and head out of town. The whole thing had definitely raised Charlie's hackles.

Of course, there is no documented evidence of the claim that one of Fry's conditions was for the town to retain Fry's name, but longtime residents say that "being nice to him" would have meant the council's total acquiescence. Fry was smart. It was never put in writing, but it has been said that he was not loathe to say now and then that the incorporation of the town was illegal. Fry filing the allegation resulted in a highly contested and expensive court battle, and allegedly was nothing more than a thinly disguised "I'll show you" revenge.

Nola Walker is shown here, c. 1944. Nola would go on to have a substantial influence on Sierra Vista. (Courtesy of Nola Walker.)

Yes, it is possible Charlie Elledge was right; if the council had accepted retaining the name Fry, the legal skirmishes might never have happened. The problem is, there's a definite difference of opinion regarding Erwin Fry. "He was friends with my Dad," says Kathy Mayo, "but I don't know that they were good friends. It was more that they liked to drink together. Erwin Fry would come over, and they'd pull out one of those—oh, what do you call it? Not a 'flask' exactly, but they all carried one in their back pocket and it was full of whiskey." Kay Mayo, shaking her head, adds "Oh, Erwin was a stubborn old man!" "And mean," says Nola Walker. "He once threatened to kill us. He said, 'If those Walkers ever set foot on my property again, I'll take a shotgun to them!' and we believed he would." Nola and her husband Charles had long been involved in the creation of the new school district and in incorporating Sierra Vista, and Nola would deliver the biggest blow to Fry's ego. She would have the final say in denying Erwin Fry the thing he wanted most: his name on the new town.

Several stories float about, purportedly telling how Sierra Vista came to bear its name. They all contain a bit of truth. None have the whole story. "I tried to tell Jac Hein [author of a narrative history, *c.* 1983]," Nola says, "but he wouldn't listen. He just brushed me off."

The truthful part is that the council (not yet officially recognized by the State of Arizona) knew that a name would be necessary to process the incorporation. Wanting a name that the majority would approve and accept, they not only talked among themselves and with friends, but seriously invited ideas from the public that summer. One version has a ham radio operator involved, who allegedly got tired of people all over the world ragging him about the name Fry, Arizona. That radio operator was Clarence Sherbundy who finally reacted, saying "I'm going to make an offer of a war bond to anyone who comes up with a better name for this town. I'm tired of telling people it's not as hot in Fry as the name implies." Up to 30 different names were suggested in response to his offer.

It is acknowledged that Charles Keller Walker suggested the name "Sierra Vista," but that's not all of the story. He sent it in, but Nola says, "I'd read that it meant 'mountain view' and I thought it was kind of a pretty name. I told him I wanted him to send in that name, and he did." Verne Hegge (still living in Sierra Vista) told Jac Hein a version only slightly modified. According to Hegge, he and a man named Swede Bergman were discussing the name over coffee and Bergman suggested "Sierra Vista." With Bergman's permission, Hegge wrote the name down an handed it in. Walker handled all the suggestions and then turned them over to the city council. "And," he says, "for all I know, it could have been Walker who mentioned the name to Bergman in the first place."

So now we have a name—Sierra Vista—first conceived of by Nola Walker, who gave it to her husband Charles, who mentioned it to Swede Bergman, who suggested it to Verne Hegge, who wrote it down and turned it back in to Charles Walker, who gave it to the city council. But this is still not the whole story.

The makeup of the Council changed during the turmoil and confusion surrounding whether Sierra Vista was legally incorporated or not. Although the first group contained women, the second (some would say more official) one did not. It consisted of five men chosen from the original list of nominations: Louis Bressnick, Paul Keating, Verne Hegge, Rudy Steffen, and C.D. Sherbundy. There were no real council offices (meetings were often held in a local club). To put the new city "in the black," each councilman donated $1 to the city treasury.

Prior to Sierra Vista's incorporation being legally recognized by the State of Arizona, Marie Pfister was named city clerk, a position she retained even after the incorporation was declared valid. She was, historically speaking, the first city clerk of Sierra Vista, although she served without an office. After all, if the incorporation wasn't legal, the city didn't exist, and if it didn't exist, it couldn't rent offices. So, there was no name on the door, no desk, no telephone, no file cabinets, nothing but Marie's briefcase and a big box she kept in the trunk of her car. It meant that when suggestions for naming the "new' city began arriving, there wasn't much of any place to put them.

Enter Nola Walker, still—as of this writing—living in Sierra Vista and still a good friend of the former city clerk, Pfister. Because there was no office, the cards with suggested names on them were put in a separate box. As a favor to a longtime friend, so Marie wouldn't have to haul it around, Nola kept the box of cards safely in a closet at home. "I was not hiding them," she says, "Everyone knew where they were."

Finally, after all the legal problems were resolved, city council members went to Phoenix for the finalization of incorporation proceedings. It was a gloriously exciting day! Would the city finally be official? Or would it not?

At home, certain people were on tenterhooks, waiting to see if the approval would be forthcoming. Finally, the phone call came; Nola picked up the receiver, identified herself, and heard the words "It's approved! All we need now is a name, and they'll sign the papers. What name got the most votes?"

Nola's favorite was and always had been the name Sierra Vista (Spanish for "mountain view," referring to a range of mountains instead of just one) after having read it somewhere; she made no secret of her preference, believing it was not only a pretty name but appropriate due to the number of mountain ranges surrounding the community. She'd just been given a golden opportunity and she was not loathe to use it. When asked the question "What name got the most votes?" the simple, unvarnished truth is that she didn't go check the cards for the latest count; she just replied "Sierra Vista." Though it probably was the name with the most votes, absolutely no one checked to see. Therefore, Nola Walker actually named the city. And that's the whole truth.

The year 1956 saw the incorporation approved, although there was that enclave within the city limits. Located in the near northwest part of the community, Fry Townsite was a holdout. Whatever his reasons for doing so, it was unfortunate for some of the people who lived and did business within the area's parameters because it condemned the small independent colony to a long downhill slide.

Given all that, Fry Townsite was home to some of the community's finest people, men and women who gave of themselves not only to their neighbors, but for the complete, overall locale. One such woman was a lady named Willie Mae Williams, also known as Granny Williams. Her husband had been one of the Buffalo Soldiers, but Granny brought religion to the community. Granny originally came from Georgia. She moved here and lived in a house on the corner of Whitton and Carmichael. She also held the first Sunday School services for kids in Fry, inviting them to her "church" in an adobe building located just about where NAPA Auto Parts/Dunkin' Donuts is today. Granny's building also hosted some of the early city council meetings.

About the same time the town was incorporated, another church was established. In 1956, the First Baptist Church met in a building on North Avenue, striking out from its mission status that was established the prior year. First Baptist is believed to be the oldest church congregation in Sierra Vista, surpassing even St. Andrew the Apostle Catholic Church.

Nola Walker is shown here as a checker at the Food Giant grocery store, no longer existent. (Courtesy of Nola Walker.)

11. Buena School District

Paul Nott, who moved to the area in 1951 and opened the fifth business establishment in town (he was the first insurance agent/broker), was both a nominee for the interim city council and an excellent lobbyist for the new school district. He once reported that because Tombstone School District wanted to keep the kids from Huachuca City and Sierra Vista in their schools, they applied to the federal government for monies to build a new high school. The federal government's Department of Health, Education, and Welfare (HEW) gave them $376,000 and somehow, they got Fort Huachuca to give them 45 acres of land. While all that was going on, Nott was traveling—at his own expense—to Washington, D.C. to lobby for a new school district belonging to Sierra Vista.

While Nott was in Washington, others back home were working hard to drum up support for the movement. There were petitions to get signed, knocking on doors to be done (so one could talk to residents), meetings to be held and attended, encouragement to flagging spirits that needed given. Through it all, Nola Walker would with her husband staunchly support the movement; they gave not only of their time but of physical effort even when others became discouraged and believed the government was simply dragging its feet, hoping they'd give up.

It is true the government had, up until then, been rather hesitant in approving the formation of a new school district. One problem was its proposed location and the question of whether, indeed, a new district was actually needed. Some folks cited the area's fluctuating enrollment which had, in the past, changed with the activation and deactivation and reactivation of Fort Huachuca; they worried it would happen again. Others considered the area a rural community that was already served quite adequately by the Tombstone School District. And some could see further down the road, figuratively speaking; looking to the future, they believed—correctly, as it turned out—that Fry/Sierra Vista was on the edge of fantastic growth and, therefore, needed its own school district. Still, getting it approved was an uphill battle.

Perhaps the legalization of Sierra Vista's incorporation gave the government the impetus it needed to approve formation of a new school district, one separate from Tombstone. Perhaps it was something else. Regardless, the new district was approved and called Buena School District #68. Its first school board members were Paul Keating, Ruth Anderson, and Marcia Weinrich; when Weinrich resigned,

It's said the "first" District Headquarters was temporarily in the same adobe building as the first Buena School. Obviously, the district needed more modern facilities and soon moved into the building shown here (photo dated April 1968). (Courtesy of Lynn Dottle, School District Headquarters.)

J. Wesley Little took her place. Paul Nott and Henry Kincaid were added, bringing the total number of elected board members to five. When Ruth Anderson's term expired, she chose not to run again; Sam Barchas was elected in her place.

The school board started out with two women; one resignation and one expiration eliminated the women and both were replaced with men, meaning the first school board was all male. The action was similar to what happened with the city council because they too nominated and appointed women to the group before incorporation, but by the time incorporation was legal, the council consisted of all men.

Not long after elections were over and the board sworn in, a gentleman named Mr. Lillywhite came out from HEW in Washington, D.C. to visit Fort Huachuca at the request of the post commander. Lillywhite's purpose was to tell folks, especially the Buena School District, that the money ($376,000) had been given to the Tombstone School District.

Sam Barchas, newest member of the board and a highly regarded (retired) attorney, made himself known. He stood up. He asked those gathered, those who had just heard that HEW gave thousands to the school district they were bucking, "Do you people want to fight this issue, to have a school of your own?" A strong "Yes" was his answer. It was all he needed. He promised, "I'm going to make the county back up, the state back up, and the federal government back up!"

With no place for personnel to live, ready-made homes came to Fort Huachuca. During the build-up, housing for Civil Service employees was almost nonexistent and construction was essential. Many were hauled in on trucks, then placed in a section called "Bonnie Blink" on Fort Huachuca. Rumors are that they came from an abandoned project in Douglas. (Courtesy of the Henry Hauser Museum.)

Joe Cracchiolo joined him in the fight for a high school for Sierra Vista. They attended a hearing in the county supervisor's office in Bisbee after which Paul Keating placed an injunction on the Tombstone School District. The injunction kept them from using any of that $376,000 for construction.

At that point, the post commander rotated and the new one was General Frank Moorman, for whom Moorman Avenue (running beside the current U.S. Post Office) is named. The general liked to form his own opinions, and so he invited Henry Kincaid to his office to explain the school situation. The outcome of that meeting was a letter dictated by another board member, Sam Barchas, that Moorman carried to Washington, D.C. When Moorman returned, he held an on-post meeting and explained that he was throwing all his influence behind the effort to establish the new school district. Three years later, Tombstone gave back the $376,000 and the army took back the 45 acres of land. Sierra Vista would have its own high school but first, there was the matter of money.

Once incorporation was official, construction of Carmichael School—named for Margaret Carmichael who donated the land—was begun, subsidized by government funds. It is in some ways a historical elementary school built in the civilian community but close to Fort Huachuca. Kids from military families went to classes there. So did children whose parents were Civil Service employees. Several of them, living in those trailers out in Huachuca City (which had formerly been known as Camp Stone, Campstone, and Huachuca Vista), moved their mobile homes to Sierra Vista so their kids wouldn't be bused to Tombstone. It was their choice, but it caused problems with overcrowding at Carmichael School. School facilities ranged from a quonset hut to a nearby church to whatever was available. Something had to be done.

Enter the Parent Teacher Association (PTA). First, members of the PTA went from door-to-door, begging people to join and attend the meetings. Some did, but most didn't. A few parents cared enough to be active and petitioned for a $68,000 bond. It died at the election. Residents of the new city didn't care enough and the bond was voted down. There was no money.

Twelve people took it seriously enough to do something about it. They were Nola and Charley Walker, Ed and Louise Bressinck, Henry and Claire Kincaid, Frank and Thalia Gregory, Gertrude and Elton Besley, Ahmad Montasser, and Garland Marrs. Frank Gregory even went to Washington, D.C. to address HEW's Mr. Lillywhite. Lillywhite was honest but not exactly complimentary. He recounted that the people of Sierra Vista had voted down the bond issue and opined that the people were not willing to help themselves. He asked "How do you expect me to do anything for you? You've got to help yourselves first."

Back home, Gregory called a joint meeting of the PTA and school board. Another petition was drawn up, this time asking for $90,000. Sierra Vista hadn't yet been official for a full year, but in December, elections took place and the bond was passed. The very next month (January 1957) HEW granted an additional $110,000 above and beyond what had been requested, for a total of $200,000. The addition to Carmichael School was built.

High school students, however, were still being bused to Tombstone. They had to get up early while it was still dark outside, and didn't get home until later, spending unnecessary hours on the road, traveling back and forth. It took a while, but the PTA finally got enough families to back them, to give them the support they needed, and they attended a meeting in Tombstone with the Union School District to discuss the matter. It was a veritable parade as assorted vehicles carrying about 100 people went from Sierra Vista to Tombstone that evening.

One man on the Tombstone board, Pete Keller, later admitted that he said, "You'll get a school district over my dead body!" He explained that he believed taxes would be raised, that Tombstone was doing the right thing by bussing all the kids over to their already-established schools. Of course, he admitted, the people near the fort wanted their own schools and he could see that but it would sure put a dent in the economy of Tombstone. They had an alternative action.

After the meeting, Tombstone met with the people of Huachuca City (to the north of Sierra Vista) and proposed a school for them. It would, they said, be built near the north gate leading onto Fort Huachuca and thus would handle all the kids from military families. It would even handle the kids of Civil Service employees who lived in Huachuca City. The proposal would have kept the schools in the Tombstone School District (as Huachuca City's schools are, even today) but again, people in Sierra Vista were looking to the future. They knew the city was destined to be more than a small community outside Fort Huachuca's gates. They could see the city's potential and saw to it that Tombstone district's proposal to build "a" school in Huachuca City was defeated. Tombstone district, on the other hand, was just as determined to hang on to what they had and continued the fight against a new high school in a little upstart city. It was a lost cause; the people of Sierra Vista were determined and of strong pioneer stock. They would not give up.

Time passed. It took another year to research information and firm up plans. Again, it involved legalities. However, armed properly, HEW was again approached and this time, Lillywhite was more amenable. He told the people from Sierra Vista that if they would get the legal things straightened out, he would grant the money to build a high school.

The PTA got busy once again. They campaigned, they circulated petitions, and they talked and talked and talked. This time, when an election was held, the people of Sierra Vista voted to withdraw from the Tombstone School District. Excitement ran high, and immediately HEW was informed of what had happened. HEW responded by giving the young city $50,000 to build a new high school. The only question was where to build it.

Andrea Cracchiolo donated land for the school, but not everyone liked the location (up near the intersection of Bypass 90 and Seventh Street). Others wanted it to be built on Seventh Street but at the southeast corner where it crosses Fry Boulevard. Some of the ones who liked that plan were the same ones who made the east-west dividing line where it is, never considering that Sierra Vista would grow. They thought, one supposes, that things would stay the same forever. Things never do.

Sierra Vista is uniquely situated. It cannot expand westward; Fort Huachuca is there. It can't really expand much northward; Huachuca City, still unincorporated today, is there and northward growth would involve swallowing that community after first getting through portions of the post. The only growth possible (then and now) is eastward and southeast. And growth was inevitable.

Thus, the new high school really should be built "out in the country," on state-owned land leased by Joe Cracchiolo. It was approved and Cracchiolo signed over 40 acres of his lease. The high school's location would be right across the street from the first Buena School, just about where Gas City is now located. And it would be called Buena High School. Something—either driveways or sidewalks—appears to remain on the premises, sort of like the remnants of an old ghost town. One can cross Fry Boulevard at the traffic light, heading north on Avenida Escuela (Spanish for "School Street"); once across, there's a choice. Turn left and you're into the School District's administrative offices. Curve to the right, down a semi-twisted path, and you are on the old high school grounds, now Gas City. That first Buena High School had maybe ten classrooms. And it wasn't in Fry, another thorn in the side of Erwin.

Buena High School's first commencement ceremony was held on May 26, 1959, with 19 graduating seniors, just a few more than the eighth grade commencement first held in the original Buena School just across the highway.

While not directly involved in the hard work required to get the school, one strong proponent of the effort was Marie Pfister. While the school controversy raged, Marie encouraged and supported, but had myriad other responsibilities to deal with, responsibilities that involved not only city business (and businesses), but most individuals who lived within the city's sphere of influence. For instance, she left her job at Fort Huachuca to open her own business, renting space just across the street from Paul Keating's service station (right outside the main gate, popular since before the days of the "Mobile Madam"). Pfister was a notary public, a good bookkeeper, and a public stenographer. The office wasn't far from her first home in the area, located behind Margaret Carmichael's home, but it was at the edge of town. Practically everything ended at Seventh Street.

Building up her one-woman enterprise, Marie began acting as collection agent for Arizona Public Service, the gas company, and the electric company. The companies would eventually have their own offices but, at the time, customers would come to Marie's to pay their bills. She also signed up new customers, accepted their deposits, and took orders for the service repairman.

An aerial view of Fort Huachuca is shown here, c. *1960. (Courtesy of the Fort Huachuca Historical Museum.)*

What most people didn't know is that Marie often carried a lot of cash with her. One problem is that the electric company—Sulphur Springs Valley Electric Cooperative (SSVEC)—didn't have a local bank account. So what Marie did was take all the money with her out to the bank on Fort Huachuca and deposit it into her personal account before transferring it to the company. Was she nervous about doing this? She admits, "Well, there were times when I was kind of uneasy about it, and I wished SSVEC would open an account for me. But they didn't, so I had to do it that way."

So back in the mid-1950s, Marie Pfister was one busy, hard-working person. In addition to running her own business, she was the secretary for the Fry Citizen's Association, and when Sierra Vista was incorporated, she became city clerk. As such, she would issue building permits. Her very first one was for the Stanley Apartments, located on the southeast corner of the intersection where South Garden Avenue meets Wilcox Drive. When the permit was issued, the land was nearly vacant, with one old storage shed on it, so Marie posted the notice on that.

Sierra Vista's first chief of police, Clarence Sherbundy, was also the man for whom Sherbundy Street is named. (Courtesy of the Henry Hauser Museum.)

She would, in years to come, hold several more positions. For instance, she was the deputy registrar for Cochise County, Buena District; as such, she handled voter registrations and worked 24-hour days on election days.

It was a relatively few short years after incorporation when Marie "retired" from her job as City Clerk, but she didn't stay retired. She went to work for the *Huachuca Herald* newspaper and an insurance agency. Somewhere along the way, Marie acquired a nickname: "Sister Pfister from Sierra Vister." Many of her old-time friends still call her that, although she did become Marie Storment upon her marriage to Frank. There are two streets in Sierra Vista named to honor Marie. They are Pfister Avenue and Pfister Place, both in the northwest (the historical) part of town.

She was definitely there at the birth of a new town/city and she watched its growing pains. One of them involved city services and where to house them; Sierra Vista couldn't go on forever operating out of the trunk of Marie's car and her briefcase. The town needed a place of its own.

Its first place was in a World War II-era quonset hut near the main gate to Fort Huachuca. The hut would eventually become Atlas Furniture, but at the time it was quite serviceable. The new council did pay $2.04 to have a sign painted saying "Town Hall" and they posted it on the building. They were in business. This didn't mean it was anywhere near state-of-the-art; manual typewriters were around, of course, but electric models weren't. Telephones existed but they were dial phones, not even pushbutton units, and answering machines did not exist. There were no computers, and topnotch adding machines had 100 keys on them (10 rows across, 10 rows down).

So temporarily, humans were taking messages, writing them down, and giving them to the intended recipient when they came by. Policemen would, every so often, stop in to see if there were any calls requesting services—a method of operation having an obvious effect on response time. Luckily, the town was still small enough it didn't take long to get to the caller's location.

Clarence Sherbundy was the first police chief; actually, he was also the town's first police officer, and an unpaid one at that. He was one of the original members of the Town Council, relinquishing that position in order to accept an appointment as the chief of police. At the time, there really wasn't any money in the treasury to pay him (remember, he was one of the five who chipped in $1 each just so the town could have an official treasury). Whether the little cash required came from that initial $5 is unknown, but what did happen is that the town had some tickets printed up. It was a beginning. Chief Sherbundy would use them to ticket illegally-parked vehicles along what is now Fry Boulevard. In addition to issuing certain business licenses, the traffic tickets were another method used by the town to generate some of its early revenue. Sherbundy stayed chief for just a few months, long enough to help get the department started and to get the funds built up so a new chief could be hired. Then Sherbundy resigned.

The second chief of police—James Wells—was actually the first paid chief and assumed his position on April 1, 1957. His starting salary was the princely sum of

$300 per month, but a few weeks later, he got a raise of $45 per month. He would stay on the job for two years before leaving to accept another position in Coolidge, Arizona. Chief Wells died of a heart attack in 1975.

He was followed by Raymond Thompson, who accepted the position but kept it for only four months before offering his own resignation on July 2, 1959. He was succeeded by Bill Stone (the fourth chief in three years); Stone would stay for three years, the longest so far. His was not a peaceful reign; supported by Police Commissioner Paul Keating, he apparently was well-liked by members of the community, but his problems were not with the people. It was with the city council: several times, they threatened to fire him and he once resigned but withdrew the resignation. On March 15, 1962, he received his last firing notice

C. Reed Vance was another chief of police in Sierra Vista. (Courtesy of the Henry Hauser Museum.)

The very first city hall is shown here, after Sierra Vista was legally formed. This building housed the police department, city offices, and more. (Courtesy of the Henry Hauser Museum.)

upon which two officers and one clerk immediately resigned. Sierra Vista certainly was having a difficult time keeping its peace officers! (It did get better: #5 stayed for 27 years, #6 retired after 13 years, #7 is currently on the job.)

During its infancy, the new town government had a number of unexpected difficulties. According to an early council member, laws and statutes pertaining to city administration are for established cities, and Sierra Vista was a mere baby. One man remembers, even today, an early statute that clearly proclaimed any year's budget cannot exceed the previous year's budget by more than 10 percent. The problem was, Sierra Vista didn't have a previous year's budget because it hadn't existed—the town was only a few months old! Well, there's a way around everything; you only have to find it. And the officials of Sierra Vista did.

One big hurdle was banking hours. Back then, banks' accepted practice was to stay open during the hours that most people were at work, closing when most people were off work. That meant they were closed evenings and weekends, a practice entirely for the convenience of the bank employees (not the customers whose money was under the bank's control). It didn't matter what one's business was nor how important the reason, when 4:00 p.m. came, banks closed. When they closed on Friday, they stayed closed until the following Monday morning. It caused a major problem for the military because, once a month, the soldiers got paid on the 1st whether it was a weekday or weekend (no computers, no direct deposit). Even if their payday fell during the week, they couldn't get off work—

nor could anyone else—to make a run to the bank before 4:00 p.m. It was a very inconvenient way to do business, but "it's always been done that way."

In a wonderful act of cooperation with the soldiers from Fort Huachuca, Paul Wolfe (who owned the Bent Elbow Bar) solved the problem. He took it upon himself to become the town's "weekend banker." Before the First National Bank closed at 4 p.m. on Friday, Wolf would withdraw $20,000 (in $5s and $10s) so he could offer check-cashing services. He kept the money in a hiding place at his store; furthermore, he slept on the premises with a loaded weapon just in case.

Come Monday morning, promptly at 10 a.m. (yes, 10 a.m.—banks were only open six hours a day), Paul Wolfe would be back at the bank the instant it opened. He would return all $20,000 plus $10 that the bank charged him for the weekend's use of the money. He didn't mind; he more than made up that $10 through business done at his store because he offered the additional service.

Those were the days—the kind of times when Paul Wolfe and Marie Pfister could carry around large sums of cash and no one bothered them (perhaps, though, that was becuase Wolfe was armed; no one has ever said whether Pfister was or not). Things were certainly different then, but they were about to start changing.

The Arizona Bank is allegedly the first full-service bank in town. It no longer exists, since the company was bought out by Security Pacific and then by Bank of America. A later bank with a very similar name was formed, but it has also gone by the wayside. (Courtesy of the Henry Hauser Museum.)

12. A Time of Many Firsts

Sierra Vista was definitely "on the move." Fort Huachuca had been stable for awhile and it was anticipated it would stay that way. The eastward growth began.

The first item after legal incorporation was, as mentioned, the Stanley Apartments building permit. Within less than a year, additional questions came up about doing business within the city limits. Before Sierra Vista was a "real" city, it hadn't been necessary to ask about things like city taxes, whether one needed a license to have a pinball machine, jukebox, or what one should do about a sewer system in view of the expanding business community (and new residential areas), or what to do about horses ambling unchecked through the community. A community airport was proposed. Then, there was a #8 Beer License issued to Doc's Chicken Roost (now defunct). A complaint was issued about Ride-A-While Stables allowing their horses free range within the city, meaning they ate whatever was handy—grass, flowers, gardens, shrubs—and left piles in yards or wherever. The city's first stop sign was erected. A building permit was issued for a bowling alley, a furniture store, and a drive-in theater. Coronado Shopping Plaza and El Coronado Motel (now the Vista Inn) were built. The first of its kind, the Coronado was a self-contained rental community with shops downstairs, apartments on the second floor, and a hotel at the corner as an end-cap.

Kathy Mayo recalls:

> I remember the Coronado. I was in school then, a young teenager, and I guess the other kids figured I was gutsy enough to—well, let me tell you about it. The planners of the motel didn't think things through. You couldn't go directly, but we could go up the outside stairs to the second floor, cross over and come down near where the vending machines were. "Vending" as in "cigarettes." So just about every day, when we got out of school, kids would give me their quarter to go buy them some cigarettes.
>
> I got caught twice. Here a policeman came, I guess checking things at the nearby bar and stuff, and I was there with my arms full of different brands of cigarettes. I had Camels and Lucky Strikes and all different kinds. But he grinned and said "You getting those for your Dad?"

These four ladies have long, strong ties to Sierra Vista and have had a great effect thereon. From left, they are: Kathy Mayo, research assistant and daughter of Slim Mayo (the "cowboy's cowboy"); Marie Storment, the first city clerk who, among other things, handled receipts for the electric company; Nola Walker, who actually was the one who named Sierra Vista; and Katherine "Kay" Mayo, widow of Slim Mayo. Standing is the author. All are part of the Landmark Gang, who meet at Pam Marr's Landmark to discuss Sierra Vista's History.

> Everyone knew my Dad, Slim Mayo, and everyone knew my Dad smoked; still, he wouldn't have wanted all those different kinds. Several were brands he wouldn't have touched! But the cop gave me an "out" and I took it; I quickly agreed that yes, the cigarettes were for my Dad and the patrolman let me go.
>
> A few weeks later, it happened again and that time, I got a sterner warning. I sort of lost interest after that, or else it was summer and kids were out of school so they didn't have a way to ask me to get smokes for them.

(At this interview, Kathy fit into a category that qualified her for membership in AARP, and her mother, Kay, was sitting next to her. The expression on Kay's face showed that it was obviously the first time she knew about her daughter's escapades with the cigarette machines at the Coronado.)

The parameters of the first subdivision built in Sierra Vista were present-day Fry Boulevard, north to Tacoma Street, west to Garden Avenue, and east to the unincorporated Fry Townsite. Busby & Carroll Construction built 144 homes in this area. No one actually knows for sure, but word is that James Carroll chose the names of the streets in the development. In so doing, he made sure no one would forget some of the early residents of the new town. For instance, Whitton Street (where the Mayos live) was named for Fred Whitton, Steffens Street was named for the first mayor, Rudy Steffens, Wolfe Street for Paul Wolfe (the "weekend banker"), Sherbundy Street for Clarence Sherbundy (the city's first police chief), James Drive for James Carroll (why not choose one street to name for himself?), etc. Later, Busby & Carroll Construction (there is a Busby Drive, but not in that development) would go on to build an addition to that first subdivision, beginning where it left off on Tacoma Street and going on to the Highway 90 Bypass.

It is definitely true that Friehage Street was named for Nellie Friehage. It is said that she was the first woman elected to the city council, according to which city council one refers. One must recall that there was an appointed council

Slim Mayo is shown teaching the little buckaroos some rope tricks. (Courtesy of the Henry Hauser Museum.)

Henry "Hank" Hauser, a Texas Aggie and golf champion, helped design part of the Fort Huachuca Golf Course, now called the Mountain View Golf Club, which is open to the public. Hauser has been councilman and later mayor of Sierra Vista, and was active in annexing Fort Huachuca. He still keeps his finger on the pulse of the city. (Courtesy of the Henry Hauser Museum.)

before legal incorporation and a somewhat different one at the time incorporation was recognized. Both influential and highly respected, Friehage was one of the women who were first nominated and appointed for city council, in 1955, when incorporation was first attempted. However, Sierra Vista was not yet legally an entity. When the Town of Sierra Vista became official, the sitting city council consisted of five men and no women.

In 1957, the first Masonic Lodge was chartered in Sierra Vista, and its first Master was Vernon Hegge (for whom Hegge Street is named). There had been a lodge in Tombstone for quite awhile and many brethren still travel Charleston Road to the meetings, but now there was one at the northeast corner of Wilcox Avenue and Garden Avenue (just across the street from the Stanley Apartments). With its establishment, it wouldn't be long till a Chapter (#51) of Order of Eastern Star followed.

In 1958, Sierra Vista constructed its first Town Hall at 400 Sherbundy; it would house the police department, fire department, court, and other city departments. The fire department, in particular, wore a second hat when the town's first library was established on the running-board of the fire truck.

A determined number of residents wanted the town to have a library, so, in true pioneer spirit, they set out to make one. This group is now called Friends of the Sierra Vista Public Library, and they collected books from anyone who could donate them. That netted them 800, but then they ran into the problem of where to stock them. The fire station came to the rescue, offering whatever assistance they could. They didn't have a room within the building, but when a member of the Friends asked, they admitted to having fire trucks with running boards. The innovative solution helped. The library was open several times each week, its hours of availability dependent on whether the fire department received a call requiring their true services elsewhere. Instead of shelves, the fire truck rolled out the front door and sat in the driveway, the books lined up on its running boards. Volunteers formed the library's entire staff and had to be quick on their feet because they were busiest when an emergency call came in and the trucks had to roll. When that happened, the books came off the running boards in a flash!

That solution couldn't last for long, though. When the library became a part of Sierra Vista, the collection was moved first to one location and then another. It ended up in a small library on Sherbundy Street. It wasn't until 1982 that the library was moved to its first stable home at 2950 East Tacoma Street. It's the very building where the Ethel Berger Center is now. The Mona Bishop Room was where events ranging from the genealogical society meetings to library business were held; now (after remodeling) it's the Henry Hauser Museum.

Seventeen years after establishing itself on Tacoma, the library moved again—all 70,000-plus volumes—to a new and very modern building located at 2600 East Tacoma. The new library was controversial from the beginning because of its outdoor artwork and building design that included a copper roof (equivalent to the copper in 105 million pennies); old-timers didn't think it fit in with other public construction but most have come to accept it.

Also, in 1958, the main street through town was not called Fry Boulevard. Starting out as a rugged, two-lane dirt road leading to Buena and Lewis Springs, it changed. By that time, it was actually part of Highway 92 (not Highway 90, as some think). The people of Sierra Vista wanted a name change, something more in line with their being a town, not a place for a state highway passing through. Lois Richards, of the *Huachuca Herald*, thought a street-naming contest would be fun, and Gene Espinoza of radio station KHFH joined in promoting the contest.

Everyone in town was invited to send in names for the street; it would be the street from where it left the main gate of Fort Huachuca, straight east to Buena School. Whoever won the contest was to get round-trip airfare plus five nights in Las Vegas, and hearing that, people got excited! The Kiwanis Club handled the contest, and suggestions came in, lots of suggestions. True to community form, things got interesting.

Students and faculty at Buena School began shouting that the street should be named Buena Highway because it led to and from the school. Others in the town didn't think so, at which point the same students and faculty circulated a petition and got signatures from 247 people in favor of that name. It prompted one citizen to remark that they should name the town "Petition City."

This vote of popular support could not be ignored, so the road was named Buena Highway. However, no prize was awarded because, with 247 signers of the petition, there was no way each of them could be given the award. Neither could it be given to one and not the others. So the prize disappeared. No one has ever been sure what happened to the prize money but, for a while, Sierra Vista did have a main street officially named Buena Highway. It would stay that way until 1961.

It has been said that Erwin Fry offered to go along with an annexation plan he had been offered (it would take in Fry Townsite) if the town renamed the main street after him. Whether or not he made that offer, at a council meeting in 1961, Louis Broitman proposed to the council that they rename the city's main street to honor Erwin Fry. After due discussion, the motion was passed and the street renamed. Now we have Fry Boulevard running from the main gate of Fort Huachuca east to a strange intersection, "strange" because no two of the four streets leading into it are the same. One is the Highway 90 Bypass, one is Highway 90, one is Highway 92, and one is Fry Boulevard.

When the town was named Sierra Vista, it was still growing and, in 1961, would change from a town to a city. It wasn't everyone's choice, but a vote was taken and by a margin of 218–112, it was done. That same year, a special election was held to form a junior (2-year) college district in Sierra Vista; Pat Goren and Brainard Page headed the committee. It would take them two years to bring the bond issue to election. It passed, but the local districts voted against it. That caused the state College Board to establish the campus near Douglas (a satellite campus has since been created in Sierra Vista and another in Benson).

In 1963, the movie *Captain Newman, MD* was filmed nearby. Gregory Peck, Angie Dickinson, Tony Curtis, Jane Withers, and Eddie Albert starred. It was actually filmed at Fort Huachuca, and one of the wranglers on hand was Slim

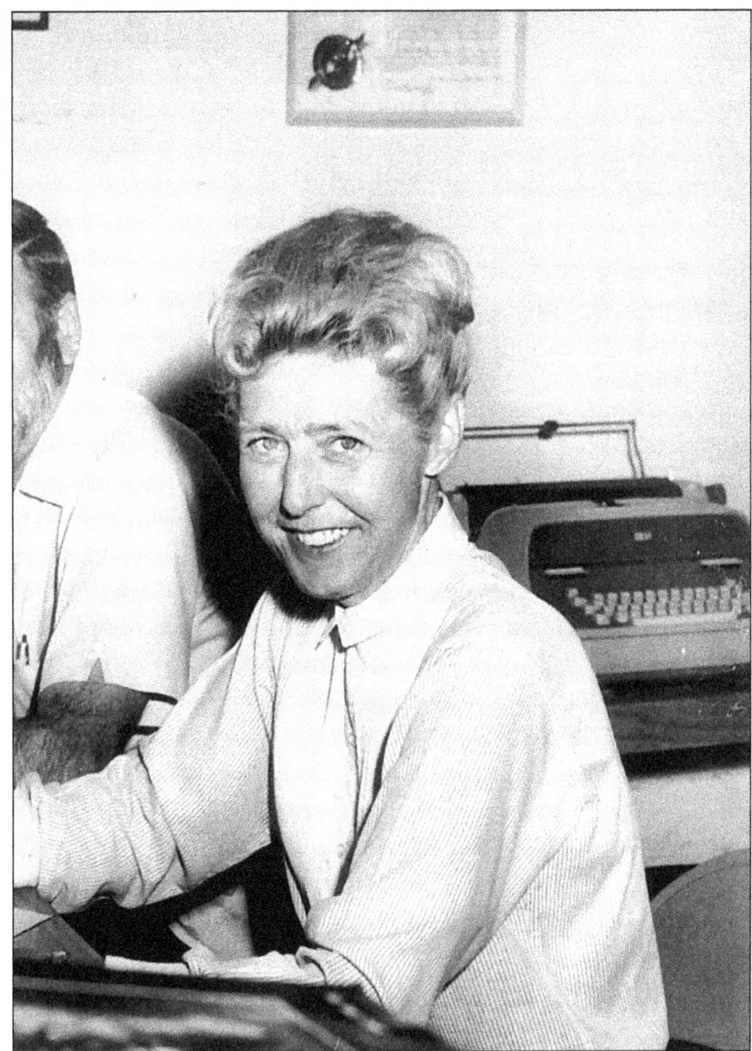

Lois Richards is shown here in her office at the first newspaper in Sierra Vista. The typewriter behind her was considered state of the art for the time. (Courtesy of the Henry Hauser Museum.)

Mayo. Most of the actors and crew stayed in town at the El Coronado Hotel (the same hotel where Kathy Mayo bought cigarettes for her schoolmates). Some of the local townsfolk signed on as extras, and others hung around to watch. There were plenty of oohs and aahs and kids who didn't want to go to school.

That same year, the Baptist Association—perhaps spurred on by the First Baptist Church—suggested opening the Cochise General Hospital. On September 6, 1963, they did; it was called the Western Baptist Hospital of Sierra Vista. Its entire medical staff consisted of Fred Patterson, chief of staff, and doctors Irving Folberg, Charles McMoran, and Delbert Mock.

As Sierra Vista grew, so did its need for additional comprehensive services. The post office that served Fry had long been closed, moved to premises still on Fry Boulevard but within the city limits of Sierra Vista. When additional residents added to its responsibilities, the post office found itself in April of 1964 relocating yet once again, from 316 East Fry to 96 South Carmichael. Still, its odyssey wasn't finished. It would move one more time to its current location at 2300 East Fry.

Around 1965–1966, the population of Sierra Vista took another downturn when the army began its buildup of troops in southeast Asia. Some have said the city was "like a ghost town," but others insist that nothing changed. Therefore, while the result may not have been extreme, Sierra Vista was somewhat affected. Businesses began closing down; a few premises sat empty. Some houses were offered for sale at very low prices. This time, it didn't last long. In 1967, what is now the Information Systems Command (ISC) was relocated to Fort Huachuca and not only single troops but army families came with it. Businesses of all different kinds, including new restaurants, opened or reopened.

The year the ISC moved to Fort Huachuca is the same year Henry Hauser was elected to the city council, a position he held until he became the mayor in 1969. Hauser retired in 1961 from the army after living in Sierra Vista for three years. Colonel Hauser had been assigned to the Army Intelligence School, where he was in charge of photo identification and interpretation. He and his wife, Jane (an "army brat"), bought one of the first houses in the brand new subdivision called Village Meadows, where they still live today. Henry (or "Hank," as he's known to friends) became an adopted son of Sierra Vista, well known and well liked on both the city council and as mayor.

The city's first government vehicle was bought secondhand and on time. It is shown here in a high-desert snowstorm. (Courtesy of the Henry Hauser Museum.)

During Hauser's tenure as mayor, he was instrumental in securing joint usage of the airport on Fort Huachuca. To the army, the airport was and still is Libby Army Air Field. To Sierra Vista, their part is the Sierra Vista Municipal Airport.

In 1972, Hank was also the driving force in Sierra Vista's successfully annexing Fort Huachuca, causing the city to grow by nearly 10,000 citizens. The city limits had jumped to 83,000 acres. Suddenly, the upstart, young city with a past had become one of the largest cities in the State of Arizona, and it happened overnight! ("Make no mistake," is the word from the Public Information Office on post, "it's still a federal reservation; the annexation was for tax purposes only." This information was confirmed by Hank Hauser.)

The man simply would not retire! There was (first) his army career and (second) his Federal Civil Service career, during which he served on the city council and as mayor. Following his term as mayor, he served on the school board, where he helped establish the tennis courts and Little Theater. He helped design the back nine holes of the Fort Huachuca Golf Course (now the Mountain View Golf Course and open to the public). When he did finally slow down a little, he assumed the mantle of historian, working tirelessly to establish the Oral History Collection for the city's museum, which is named for him.

As in any community, it is a given that some businesses start, some change hands, some relocate, some close. Through all its ups and downs, it was no different for Sierra Vista. For instance, back during World War II a USO Club had been built outside the main gate, on the south side of Fry Boulevard. (The very patriotic and generous Margaret Carmichael tried to donate the land she owned for the club, and that led to an amusing but very legal transaction. The government couldn't accept a gift such as this one, so they reached an agreement: the U.S. Treasury sent Carmichael a check for $1 as payment in full for the property.) Regulations had been served and everyone was happy. The club, built to serve the troops, sat idle during the times the post was deactivated. It was rescued by Major General Emil Lenzner (for whom Lenzner Avenue is named), who had it reopened as a Non-Commissioned Officers (NCO) Club. That didn't sit too well with the owners of two nearby clubs, and they let it be known. To keep peace in the community, Lenzner abandoned the operation off-post and built an NCO Club on-post, converting the first facility into what was called a "Service Club" until the on-post NCO Club could be built. The general offered the first building to Sierra Vista, to be used as a town hall and meeting rooms. Unfortunately, since the town had already started construction of a town hall at 400 Sherbundy Street; they declined the general's offer.

It would not go idle forever. Tony Shaieb and Roger Barnett—either of whom could write their own colorful story—teamed up to buy the Service Club and turn it into the Landmark Restaurant. Tony, now living mostly at the Lifecare Center in Sierra Vista, admits that the building was in terrible shape when he and Roger bought it. They didn't, he says, know what they were going to do with it but after talking it over, Tony decided to make it into a restaurant. Tony and his wife Val stripped out the building, painted and scrubbed and decorated. The equipment

This artist's rendition of the old Landmark before it burned shows its charm. On the south side of Fry Boulevard, not far from the Main Gate of Fort Huachuca, it has been reincarnated as a desert-pink courtyard center with a restaurant, offices, and shops. It also hosts the annual West End Fair. (Courtesy of Ricardo Alonzo.)

came from another restaurant down the street after it closed. A little later, Tony bought out Barnett and operated the Landmark himself. He was in business!

It was a glorious facility, popular with both soldiers and civilians, with good food and dancing and almost everything a body could want—until a huge, roaring fire destroyed it all. But, once everything was settled, the Landmark would rise again as if it were the legendary phoenix. This time, it would be different. It would be a one-story plaza with stucco buildings painted desert pink.

On June 21, 1975, history was made in Sierra Vista, history that would eventually spread around the world and give millions a way to zip through a meal. On that date, McDonald's restaurant opened the first ever drive-thru in Sierra Vista on Fry Boulevard just west of Coronado. The event brought incredible newspaper coverage and long lines of automobiles filled with customers excited that they no longer had to actually park, get out of the car, and go inside to eat. For awhile, the restaurant even closed its lobby doors to make it easier for customers to notice the drive-thru window—as if anyone could miss the hoopla. Bumper stickers were issued, red words on a white background, declaring "I MADE HISTORY," then in slightly smaller letters, "Sierra Vista" and "McDonald's" with the appropriate logo.

The menu board quoted fewer items and lower prices than now. For instance, when the drive-thru opened, Big Macs were 75¢, shakes were 35¢, French fries were a quarter (large size, 40¢), a hamburger was 30¢, and a cheeseburger was 35¢. Sodas—Coca-cola, root beer, or orange—were 20¢ and 25¢, milk cost a quarter, and coffee was 15¢. (In the late 1990s, that historic restaurant kept doing business while a newer, more modern facility was built right next door on the east side;

This is the dining area inside the old Landmark, where families were always welcome or a gentleman and his lady—perhaps dressed for the occasion—could enjoy a romantic evening out. (Courtesy of Pam Marr.)

This is the bar area inside the old Landmark. It was, perhaps, a little noisier and a little smokier than the dining area but stopped short of being called rowdy. Lunchtime often found many a business deal worked out between community movers and shakers. (Courtesy of Pam Marr.)

when it opened, the old building, featuring the first ever drive-thru, was torn down. The space is now the current McDonald's parking lot.)

Another milestone was reached two years later when, on January 27, 1977, Cochise College broke ground for its new Sierra Vista campus. (40 acres of land on Charleston Road, just east of the Highway 90 bypass, had been donated by the Cracchiolo family. The college's Andrea Cracchiolo Library is named in honor of the family patriarch.) Prior to the new campus opening, students attended classes in portable buildings placed on the grounds at the old Buena High School or at Fort Huachuca. As soon as the premises were ready, the portables were relocated to the new campus and three permanent buildings added. The first classes began in January 1978.

The first college president was Maryly VanLeer Peck. The first student government president was Betty Bernheim. Betty, who still lives in Sierra Vista, was 53 years old when the campus opened, but she didn't let that stop her; always hungry for knowledge, she would enroll in classes at the new campus for the next 25 years.

Other changes involved land (also south of Fry Boulevard) that was once owned by Fred Baumkirchner and his family. He came to the area in a rather roundabout way. While he and his brother were doing business in Benson, they started

On January 2, 1974, Sinew Riley Barracks at Fort Huachuca was named to honor one of its most devoted Indian scouts. Shown here are his family members, from left to right: (front row) Lillian Pablos and Peela Quintera Riley, who was Sinew's widow; (back row) Freddie, Felix, Jerry, Startt, Jimmie, and Larry, all sons of Sinew Riley. (Courtesy of the Fort Huachuca Historical Museum.)

investing in property nearer the Mexican border. It was called the Baumkirchner Brothers Ranch, eventually evolving into the Los Lomas Cattle Company. Also, they decided to relocate from Benson to this area. They rented a little shack from Erwin Fry and turned it into a bar. Business was so good, they bought the property around it and expanded, calling it the Military Inn. And they bought the original property from Fry because, Fred once said, " . . . we were paying him too much in commissions!" Years later, it would be sold to Bill Wong and turned into a Chinese restaurant, and today, it's where the Wells Fargo Bank is located. Sears moved into the store on Fry Boulevard where Furniture Impressions is now located; they would relocate to the big Mall at Sierra Vista when it was built out on Highway 92. Others didn't fare as well. Montgomery Ward, Ben Franklin, and McCrory's are national names that came and went.

Originally, a family named Hilburn contracted with Erwin Fry to build a "strip center" east of Second Street. They owned or built a number of other stores; most of them are now gone, stores such as Uncle Sam's Restaurant, Montgomery Ward, etc. One that is still here is the Village Inn Motel on the southeast corner of Fry Boulevard and Moorman Avenue, just across the street from the newest U.S. Post Office. There's a restaurant with the motel, a place now called the Rustic Rail but formerly a Sambo's Restaurant (Sambo's was a chain restaurant that fell on hard times due in part to its very name, when that name became politically incorrect.)

At the time it was built, most residents of Sierra Vista thought the Hilburns were crazy. The place was way out in the country, in the middle of nowhere. Predictions were that the Hilburns would fall flat on their faces. They didn't. The town grew out to meet them and then went past them. The motel/restaurant complex currently belongs to Sandy and Ed Weymer.

Restaurants, in particular, seem to come and go. One that came in the early 1970s and stayed is the Dunkin' Donuts on the north side of Fry Boulevard. On the other hand, a Village Inn Pancake House located itself just west of the newest post office; it is gone and a hair salon shares the building with a wireless service. Across the way, there's a Denny's that once was a Hobo Joe's. My Place, further west on Fry, was earlier the Caffe O' Le II (Caffe O' Le I is still in business, in Haymore Plaza) and before that, went through several other identities. Golden China was once across the street from where it is now. The Beef Baron, once a Ponderosa Steakhouse, has most recently reincarnated itself as the New China Buffet & Sushi Bar.

One location has suffered an unusual fate: some residents think the restaurant on the southeast corner of Fry Boulevard and Avenida Escuela is jinxed. It started out as a Bonanza Steakhouse and when that closed, it became a nightclub (name unknown). At one point, according to Kathy Mayo, it was a King's Table Restaurant. Some say there was an Italian restaurant in there somewhere, but that has not been confirmed. What is known is that there was a Mexican restaurant called Tres Amigos. When it closed, some food service employees got together and opened their own place at that location. It didn't last too long before closing, then another group opened another restaurant. That incarnation seemed to have possibilities (according to one winter visitor, they had real, pink tablecloths, and real silverware, not the cheap stuff, and the servers wore starched white jackets.) For unknown reasons, that didn't work either and they closed after a few months. The next opening was for a mesquite broiler type of bar and grill called Chuy's, featuring what they called "Killer Chicken." Chuy's didn't last a very long time before closing. It remained closed several months before reopening, again named Chuy's but with entirely different management. That time, it lasted less than a year before closing. As of this writing, the facility again sits empty.

Others that have migrated instead of simply closing include businesses located in a shopping center east of Seventh Street. Built in July of 1957, its main stores have been K-Mart, Safeway, and Thrifty Drug. The same year, Grants Department Store opened on the south side of Fry Boulevard; three years later, in 1980, K-Mart moved from its initial location and replaced Grant's. K-Mart eventually built their own new store on the north side of Fry, where they are currently located. When they moved from their former location, Basha's Mercado (groceries) moved into the building. In the same complex as Basha's, there were AutoZone and Factory-2-U; of the three, only AutoZone remains. Most of the center remains empty although there are signs that a 99 Cent store is moving into the former Factory-2-U.

Factory-2-U relocated to the Indian Hills Plaza and Basha's reinvented itself upon moving from the 800 East Fry address to Indian Hills; it became Food City. Safeway had already moved from its original location, going east, and was firmly ensconced at 2190 East Fry. Vinny's New York Pizza, which saw one of its employees win the world's Pizza Toss Championship, migrated from its home on the south side of Fry Boulevard to a new facility, built especially for the restaurant, on Highway 92.

Thomas Home Furnishings, who sold La-Z-Boy products, has closed, but a new Laz-E-Boy Furniture Showcase is open around the corner on Highway 92. The space on West Fry Boulevard where Thomas formerly held sway has reopened and is still a furniture store. On Willcox, we have the Life Care Center; nearby, on the north side of Willcox just east of El Camino Real, few newer residents would recognize the medical offices as a former one-story apartment complex.

The King's Table, Ponderosa, and others may have gone but new chain restaurants—such as Chili's and the Outback Steakhouse—are in town. Some come. Some go. Some want to tear down the old "Badluck Corner" and build an International House of Pancakes in its place.

Neither Van's Drive-In nor Sue's Drive-In are still around. Gigi's Ladies Ready-to-Wear is gone. The Green Top burned. The Geronimo Drive-In Theater is no longer with us. Even Keating's Garden Canyon Service Station is a thing of the past, entirely gone so newer residents rarely know it existed. And, says Kathy Mayo, there was once a race track in the northwestern part of town.

Some change is good, a sign of progress. Such a one occurred just a year after St. Andrew's was declared a parish. That's the year (1980) when First Baptist dedicated new facilities at 1447 South Seventh, having outgrown its initial home.

The King's Table Restaurant was one of the chains that were in the city for awhile, but didn't last. (Courtesy of the Henry Hauser Museum.)

Though it moved, it did not destroy its former home and said former home would not, comparatively speaking, stay vacant for long.

By April 1983, Shiloh Christian Center was firmly established at the North Street address where First Baptist had been. Shiloh would have a sanctuary, a school with all 12 grades, and a congregation that grew so large, it held dual services (one in Spanish). It sponsored and continues to sponsor some rather innovative fundraisers, events such as their annual "trash-a-thon" in which participants earned donations based not on the mileage walked, but on the number of bags of trash picked up along community roadways. "It's a win-win-win situation," says one who asked to remain anonymous. "Number one, we do the fund-raising thing; number two, we get exercise; and number three, the city looks better when we get done picking up trash."

Even Buena High School, on Fry Boulevard west of today's Highway 90 bypass, for which the people had to fight so hard, is no longer in its first location; when established, everyone thought it was "way out in the country." The building—another piece of history—was torn down. Now, the acreage where it was built is somewhat divided. A large part remains empty and available, but the more lucrative corner is home to Gas City, which was itself quite controversial because a certain contingent didn't want the bright lights and red signs. Buena High School is now further out in the country, in what has become an academic complex with both Cochise Community College and the University of Arizona, South, nearby. The original—and very historical—Buena School (not the high school), located on the east side of what is now the Highway 90 bypass, was also razed in the 1990s; the good news is that pieces of it remain in the possession of private citizens because the bricks that formed the walls of the school were sold to members of the community as a fundraiser. On the premises where it stood, the land donated by Paul Knoles's ancestor, are a Chili's restaurant and a Target.

A young Sierra Vista wins the State Fair's first prize for its booth sponsored by the Chamber of Commerce . Accepting the trophy are (left to right): Mary Baumkirchner, Jeannie Gonseth, Bob Lowe, Betty Jo Lowe, Vivian Montoya, John Willis, and (kneeling) Guy Mandigo on October 31, 1973. (Courtesy of Henry Hauser Museum.)

13. Was, Is, and Will Be

As in other cities, Sierra Vista will continue to grow, change, and evolve. There is crime, of course, but there has always been crime or else, there would not have been that second hanging at Fort Huachuca. The difference now is that crimes are carried out differently. On July 19, 1992, an Arizona Ranger was shot and killed while on duty; he was serving as escort to a man making a deposit in the night-deposit box at First Interstate Bank (another facility no longer here) and was shot in the head by a man who had just robbed another customer using the outside ATM. The culprit was caught and prosecuted. The bank customers survived, the Ranger did not.

Sierra Vista has graffiti, a sign of gangs establishing their territory, but in the 1990s, the City of Sierra Vista established a Graffiti Abatement Program. One of the most active members is former mayor Carl Frieders, who uses his daily walk of several miles to scope out conditions in the community, to find where graffiti may have popped up, and help see that it is eliminated as soon as possible.

Sierra Vista has parks, probably more of them per capita than most other cities. At last count, no fewer than 16 parks and facilities existed within city limits. Some are children's playgrounds, some are linear "walking" parks. For instance, two are children's playgrounds and at least eight others feature a playground as part of their focus. There are at least five with walking paths; two have basketball courts, three have softball diamonds, and one has a fitness center. The Ethel Berger Center is home to the Henry Hauser Museum, an activity room, a stage, a kitchen and dining room, a dance studio, and a horseshoe pit outside. The Oscar Yrun Community Center houses activity rooms, an auditorium, an arts-and-crafts studio, and shuffleboard and tennis courts outside. The Youth Center has pool and ping pong tables, air hockey and video games, and a lounge with a big screen television. With this abundance of things to do, perhaps Sierra Vista is most proud of its aquatic center (named "The Cove") with a party area, a wave pool, lap and competition lanes, a warm water pool, a tube water slide, a children's lagoon, a snack bar, changing rooms, diving pool, and sunning decks. All this is within the jurisdiction of the city's Parks and Leisure Department whose director is John Startt.

Ethel Berger, elected to the city council in 1971, was instrumental in acquiring land for Veteran's Memorial Park (the large one on the north side of Fry Boulevard where elaborate activities take place) before being elected mayor in 1973. Berger

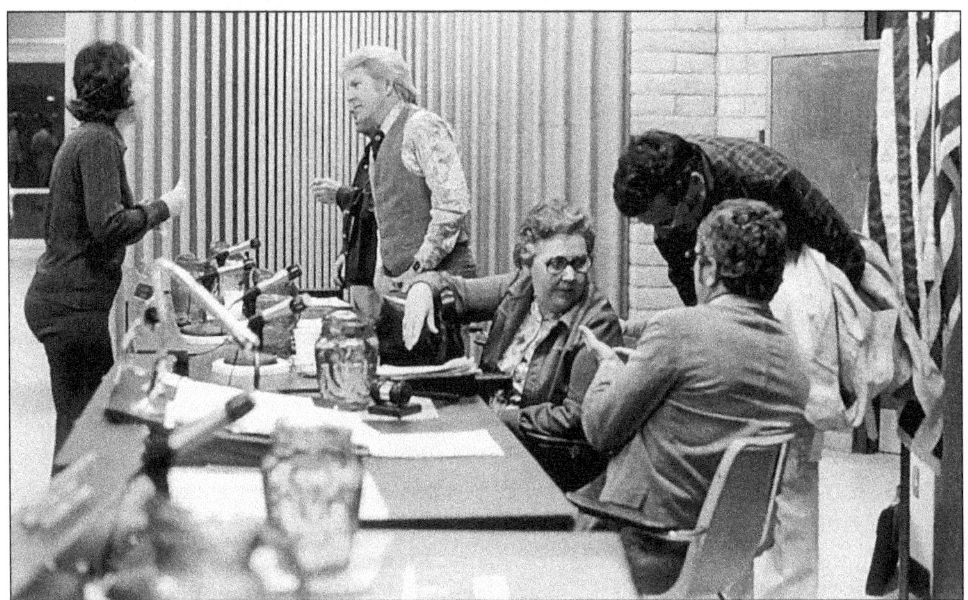

Fort Huachuca's City Council attends a meeting in this picture in the Oscar Yrun Community Center. From left to right are unidentified, Jay Raschke, Chuck Balzarini, Mikki Waddell, Mayor John Brown, Carl Freiders, and Marlis Davis. (Courtesy of the Henry Hauser Museum.)

was the first female mayor in the entire state of Arizona, opening the door for others to follow. One example was former mayor Jean Randle, after whom Jean Randle Way—leading into Veteran's Memorial Park—is named. Berger continues to be involved in more city activities and serves on more boards than you "can shake a stick at."

The city also has an unusual number of parades, beginning with the annual Holiday Parade before Christmas. There are pet parades and special-event parades. One of the most memorable, during the first Gulf War, found not only the military taking part but ordinary citizens, including one grandma pushing a stroller with a small child in it; affixed to the stroller was the sign "God bless Mommy AND Daddy in the Gulf War." There is "Art in the Park" and there is "Cars in the Park." Art in the Park takes place annually in Veteran's Memorial Park and features the work of mixed media (fine) artists, entertainment by performing artists, food booths where one can sample a variety of ethnic foods, craft sale booths with products that range from exotic jellies and jams to prize-winning carvings, and just about anything one can think of in between. It's just about the biggest such event in southeastern Arizona, helps support the Huachuca Art Association, and awards scholarships to deserving and talented students. Cars in the Park is also an annual event that takes place in the same location at a different time and attracts both participants and visitors who travel hundreds of miles just to be in the show. There are beautifully restored antique automobiles on display,

Jean Randle, former mayor of Sierra Vista, was given the honor of having a street named after her: Jean Randle Way, which leads directly into Veterans Memorial Park. (Courtesy of the Henry Hauser Museum.)

Ethel Hart Berger, the city's own councilwoman and mayor, was the first woman in the state to be elected mayor of any city. (Courtesy of the Henry Hauser Museum.)

some that aren't quite antique but definitely are classic, and some that are simply the obvious love of someone's life. Sierra Vista boasts an amazing assortment of programs and classes sponsored by the Parks and Leisure Department, a Boys' Chorus and a Girls' Chorus, a Performing Arts Center, the Ramsey Canyon Preserve (a birdwatcher's paradise famous worldwide for its incredibly rich varieties), the Folklore Center (where western folklore is collected and retained, and where limited shows feature Dolan Ellis, the State of Arizona's Official Balladeer), the Huachuca Art Association, interpretive walks along the San Pedro, and more. There's the Cochise Community College and a satellite campus of the University of Arizona.

There has been talk about establishing a Taming of the West Museum, to the point of hiring a consultant; though the idea seems to have gone by the wayside, it was originally planned for 5 acres of Fort Huachuca at the intersection of Buffalo Soldier Trail and Wilcox Drive. Instead, the entrance to the golf course on Fort Huachuca—the one Henry Hauser helped design—has been reconfigured so that non-military can play without entering the active military post. Similarly, the new

Slim Mayo was the "Cowboy's Cowboy." His weathered face was typical of the breed, as was his dry wit and his credo of living by what he considered right and wrong. (Courtesy of the Henry Hauser Museum.)

Veterans' Cemetery is built on what was Fort Huachuca land; now its entrance is on Buffalo Soldier Trail. There are plans to establish a joint information center, shared by Sierra Vista and Fort Huachuca, near the intersection of Fry Boulevard and Buffalo Soldier Trail.

Not content with cleaning up Fry Townsite, there is talk of reinventing the West End as a historical "Old Town" type of tourist attraction. If it is ever done, one of the first projects could be the Sierra Vista Western Museum, another project once in the works and separate from both the Henry Hauser Historical Museum and the abandoned Taming of the West Museum. The Sierra Vista Western Museum's first nominee should be the late Slim Mayo, a man often called a "cowboy's cowboy." Slim was transplanted from Oklahoma, working first at the Little Outfit Boys' Ranch. Kids loved him so much that they drew from all over to stage a reunion honoring Slim just a week before his death.

Slim served in the army during World War II, spending time in the Horse-Drawn Field Artillery and training troops for what was called a "Mule Pack," which is exactly what it sounds like—a line of mules (often called a pack train) under the control of the troops who used them to transport items across the rugged terrain. Interestingly, Slim was in charge of a huge herd of buffalo that was turned out to roam the unpopulated portion of Fort Huachuca. In addition to the Little Outfit, he spent time at the Sands Ranch and the Y-Lightning Ranch where his worries mainly centered on whether there had been enough rain to grow feed for the animals. He was a member of the Southwest Arizona Pioneer Cowboy's Association, the Cochise County Sheriff's Posse, and was a multiple nominee for the National Cowboy Hall of Fame in Oklahoma City, a singular honor for Cochise County because only the best are nominated. Slim was one of the best and, though born elsewhere, was an adopted son of Cochise County.

Slim is now at peace in Black Oak Cemetery, resting among friends (qualifying by courtesy of his daughter, Kathy Mayo, who was born in the area). His grave is decorated with small items pertaining to his lifestyle: a ceramic boot, plaster horses, a miniature coiled rope, and—courtesy of someone with a good sense of humor—a small tin bucket with an individual-size whiskey bottle in it. When Slim died, it was asked that in lieu of flowers, donations be made to a memorial fund through Hatfield Funeral Home; its purpose is to preserve the memory of the Little Outfit and to start the Sierra Vista Western Museum.

We must not forget the still uniquely symbiotic relationship between Fort Huachuca and Sierra Vista. An example is what some call "the Year of the Fires," when a campfire in the mountains (set, it's said, by illegal immigrants) became a raging inferno called the Ryan Fire. The wildfire scorched a massive 38,182 acres! Residents of the area breathed smoke as they went about their daily business, and the flames appeared to be less than a mile away from the main drag in Huachuca City. Men, dressed in proper firefighting gear, kept their fire trucks standing at the ready—some with engines running—in the parking lot in front of the fire station.

Fort Huachuca suffered from the effects of the Ryan Fire. The fire ignored fence lines and borders, and personnel on post scrambled to keep the flames from the electronics and other facilities. Horses kept at the Buffalo Corral were herded further away to a baseball field on the eastern side of the post (the horses loved it; there was water and fresh grass). Visitors staying in their RVs at the army's "FamCamp" had to vacate, forming a near parade around the bypass before some turned east on Charleston Road, some on Highway 90. Meanwhile, the fire raged on. West of the post, it burned through a wooden utility pole and cut off electricity. Generators kicked in everywhere except the warehouse and sales floor of the Post Commissary; there, no refrigeration meant spoilage was about to occur, perhaps hundreds of thousands of dollars' worth.

Cyndi Padgette, store manager of the commissary, was on duty within short minutes and, since the phones still worked, called around to find some help. The city responded. Padgette says:

> The people from Fry's Grocery Store, downtown, sent some refrigerated units (like on an 18-wheeler, minus the cab) so we called in people to hurry frozen items and meat into them. We didn't pay too much attention to organization, we just got it in there and stacked everything to keep it frozen. Or chilled, as the case may be. We did lose some ice cream. We thought we'd lose the fresh fruit and veggies but Tucson Produce came down and took most of that stuff, storing it in their chilled warehouse until we could clear things out and bring it back. I'll tell you, we couldn't have done it without people from Sierra Vista.

In other ways, too, the cooperation is firm between the post and the city. The Mountain View Black Officer's Club is no longer a viable facility, but the hangars at Libby Army Air Field are frequently opened to host entertainment (everything from rock music to comedians), which civilians can attend; to do so, the army makes sure the facility is properly set up, closes off some streets, directs traffic, etc. Tickets are sold at supermarkets and other stores in town. Everyone wins.

The Mountain View Black Officer's Club that in the 1940s hosted Dinah Shore and other big-name stars was still open in the mid-1970s. Visiting sisters whose parents still live in the city agree:

> We remember it. When we first came here with Mom and Dad, we were 14 and 16 years old. Dad had retired from the Army, so we were checking out the post. As teenagers, we definitely missed our telephone so when we saw a bank of phones outside the Club, we had to use them. We didn't know anyone here to call, so we just each picked up a phone and talked to each other—it didn't matter that we'd been traveling in the same car, sharing the back seat, for days. What was important was the telephone.

The Club has been empty for a long time. The Association of Buffalo Soldiers is trying to restore it as a historical building because it is the first and only club

This is the entrance to the Black Oak Cemetery where many area pioneers—with names like Pyeatt and Mayo—are taking their final rest. (Courtesy of Ron Price.)

ever built specifically for the black soldiers in a segregated army. Whether it will happen or not is questionable.

The army and the civilians have at least one other thing in common. Sort of. On Pyeatt's ranch, there's a cave that has never been fully explored. Those who have been inside a short distance say it's black as pitch and dangerous; one can toss a rock from where one is standing and listen—the rock may bounce off the walls before it splashes down, or one may never hear it land, leading some to suggest the cave may be bottomless. There are branches off the main passage of Pyeatt's Cave, twisting and turning, better than any maze. Some say there is a secret passage into Mexico, one used by the Apaches to escape after many a raid. Legend has it that Geronimo was once chased by U.S. Army troops into the very mouth of the cave, whereupon he simply disappeared from view before showing up a little later in Mexico. Some say it's been used by drug runners and possibly it has. The one certainty is that it holds many dark secrets waiting to be discovered.

One potential secret has evolved from something that happened in 1908; it concerns two explorers, soldiers from Fort Huachuca, who rode horseback to the mouth of Pyeatt's Cave. The young men carefully followed recommended safety precautions. They tied the horses to a tree—probably mesquite—near the entrance, then went inside, carrying candles, matches, chalk, and string. The soldiers did not come out. The next morning, the horses were located and led back to the stables. A search party formed, but the soldiers were never found. The post commander checked everywhere, talking to friends and family but he discovered nothing. What happened to the soldiers or their bodies? Will they ever be found? Is there an exit at the end? The cave is still there, but was the exit into Mexico destroyed in the big earthquake? Just how big is the cave? No one knows its size for sure, nor where the passageways lead. Perhaps someday a curious spelunker will find out, but until then, it remains a mystery.

Fort Huachuca also has a cave, or maybe it isn't what it seems. A hiker, a soldier named Jones, fell into a cave off Huachuca Canyon, disappearing instantly from his companion's sight. At the bottom of the cavern, Jones dusted himself off and looked around; there was a tunnel leading to a large "room." In it, Jones found stacks and stacks of gold bars measuring 16 by 4 by 2 inches. In events paralleling those of the more famous Lost Dutchman, Jones got himself out of the hole with the help of his friend and they ran down the mountain to report the find, but no one believed them. (In the Superstition Mountains, Jacob Walz discovered a fabulously rich vein of gold, but hid it till he could file his claim. Perhaps he hid it too well, for although he had a sample of the ore, he never found his way back to the mine's location. Chilling legends have developed about the mine, books have been written, and still—even to this day—fortune hunters come to search for the Lost Dutchman Mine.)

Jones returned, breaking off a piece of gold to prove his claim. Then, so it would be easier to locate, he carved his initials into a rock and placed it beside the entrance to the cave. He claimed to have carried the chunk to a nearby town to have it assayed, but no record exists that he had. If he did, it was probably kept secret because having gold in certain quantities was made illegal as part of the law enacted when the United States went off the gold standard in 1933. Anyway, Jones

The old Fort Huachuca Cemetery was one of the first things in place when the original post was established. In one corner, there are the graves of two hanged men, which seem to mysteriously draw visitors' attention.

couldn't store all the gold he had discovered in his barracks, so he temporarily left it where it was; it had been hidden for years, so a little longer wouldn't matter. Having something assayed to determine its value has nothing to do with where it was found—it's like having a diamond ring appraised; one can get an appraisal without saying where the ring came from. So they waited. During the waiting period, his buddy died and no one else knew where the gold was. There would be no split; Jones would have it all!

After Jones was discharged from service, he discovered a problem. Now a civilian, he was no longer as free to roam around the army post as he had been. It took nearly two decades, but he finally got permission to go back into Huachuca Canyon and search. Once there, he noticed that things were the same but somehow different. Was it the monsoons, when water came crashing down the mountains? Was there something moved? Jones started digging, after several hours asking the army engineers for help. They sent a bulldozer. Not too far down, the bulldozer hit water and the walls started caving in. The bulldozer operator covered it over and went away. Still, Jones wouldn't give up. He had seen the gold and knew it was there.

He persisted. Again, the U.S. Army agreed to help. This time, word had circulated and there were visitors: the army, several civilians, some treasury officials. A local television station had its mobile unit standing by. All that came up was oozing black mud. After awhile, the watchers lost interest, and just about dusk, the big shovel hit solid rock. They finally gave up, but Jones didn't. He returned with a contractor, even a spiritualist who claimed to have a vision. The gold was never found. Is it another Lost Dutchman? Is the gold there, buried somewhere on a mountain up Huachuca Canyon? Who knows?

So there is history here. It all depends on how one defines the term. As for the City of Sierra Vista, history is there, too. Fry's house, originally built about where the Dollar Store is now, had been standing empty for a long time and was being considered for use as a museum, but it burned down before anything positive could happen. No one knows for sure, but the consensus is that vagrants or illegal immigrants were camping out inside and managed to set fire to it.

The original Carmichael Store, where they had the Garden Canyon post office, is still standing; a historical building, one of a mere handful that remain, it has gone through several changes from the time when the Carmichaels established it and the Frys leased it. It was, among other things, Bill's Trading Post and the Stronghold Restaurant before its current incarnation as Daisy Mae's Steakhouse. Carmichael House, on Garden Avenue where Margaret Carmichael lived, has been turned into a real estate office, but there is some talk of trying to secure it as a historical building to be home to the museum.

Fry Townsite is finally being cleaned up. The railroad no longer runs through the center of town (although some of the tracks still exist). It has long been assumed by many that Erwin Fry, upon his death, was buried in Fry Cemetery. Actually, he wasn't. Bitter at his perceived treatment by the people of Sierra Vista, he had the last laugh on them. Kathy Mayo investigated and learned that Erwin

Is it a ghost? During an annual "cleansing" at Fry Cemetery in Fry Townsite, this apparition rose from its grave. First thought to be a dust-devil, opinion is that it couldn't be, since there was no wind, not even a breeze. Furthermore, it has happened several more times, although this is the first time it was photographed. (Courtesy of the Henry Hauser Museum.)

Fry had been cremated and, at his request, his ashes were flung to the four winds from atop Carr Peak. Therefore, he is still here somewhere.

Fry cemetery was started way back when Oliver Fry first established a home and several businesses. It was, first and foremost, a family plot. However, a lot of (unnamed) people are buried there, many of them the unwanted babies of women who worked in White City. It is also the burial place of several poor families, people who had no money for a regular funeral nor for a headstone. "Old Man Fry" (as they called him) and later his son, Erwin, let them have space to lay a loved one to rest. Some of them are not only unnamed, but unmarked.

The cemetary has been up for sale in recent years; one businesswoman wanted to turn part of it into additional parking (upon which one angry widow had her late husband dug up and moved to Cochise Memory Gardens). There's at least one resident ghost, discovered when St. Andrew's Church held an annual "cleansing" ceremony. Nola Walker discovered the ghost, clearly shown on pictures she had taken. She says:

> There it was, an apparition coming straight up from one of the graves. It was sort of like a thin cloud; at first, I thought maybe it was a "dust devil" but there was no wind. Not even a breeze. Nothing to stir it up. Several of us were standing close, but we felt nothing. Yet, it appears in at least three pictures. I think it was trying to tell possible buyers to go away, to leave them alone.

Is it a ghost? Maybe. There is one that haunts Carleton House, the oldest building on Fort Huachuca and originally a hospital. After being used as a hospital, it's been a home, an officer's mess, post headquarters, a café, a schoolhouse, and a vacation retreat for two governors of Arizona. Carleton House's ghost was experienced by an early commander of the U.S. Intelligence Center, but several other residents have encountered it, too. In fact, the ghost has a name: Charlotte. Charlotte appears rarely, and it's assumed she was a lady who probably died in the hospital when it was new. No one knows for sure; what they do know is that strange things have happened. Details can be found on the internet of an account written and copyrighted by Troy Taylor.

So Fort Huachuca has its ghost, and now Sierra Vista has discovered that they have a resident ghost, too. The latter has frightened off more than one possible buyer for the property, but not the city, who wants to acquire it as a historical site. Perhaps that would be the proper use for it.

The people of Sierra Vista are waking up to the fact that yes, they do have a history. Struggling for so long to grow the city, they have—for some time—not felt the urgency to retain their stories or their buildings. Hank Hauser did his part by taping numerous oral histories; he is now ready to retire from the self-imposed assignment and is in the midst of turning over the reins to his replacement. To use a cliché, "time marches on," and history will continue to be made.

This alternate view of the same event shows that the apparition is rising directly from the grave. Some say the spirits are disturbed at the property being placed for sale. (Courtesy of the Henry Hauser Museum.)

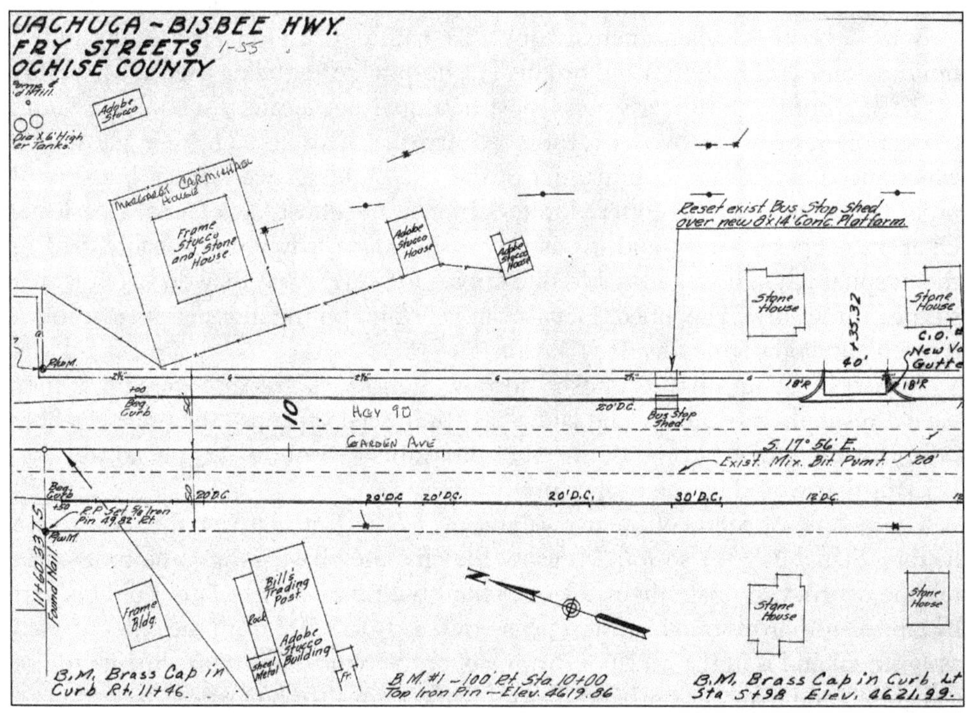

Number 1 in a set of six city street maps, annotated by K. Mayo. (Courtesy of Kathy Mayo and J. Herrewig.)

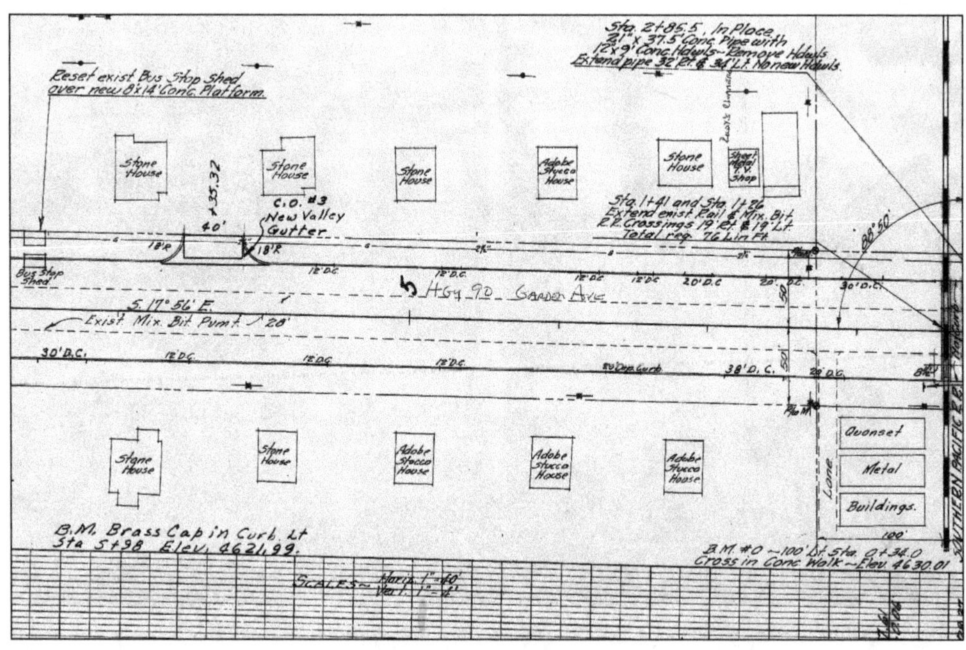

Number 2 in a set of six city street maps, annotated by K. Mayo. (Courtesy of Kathy Mayo and J. Herrewig.)

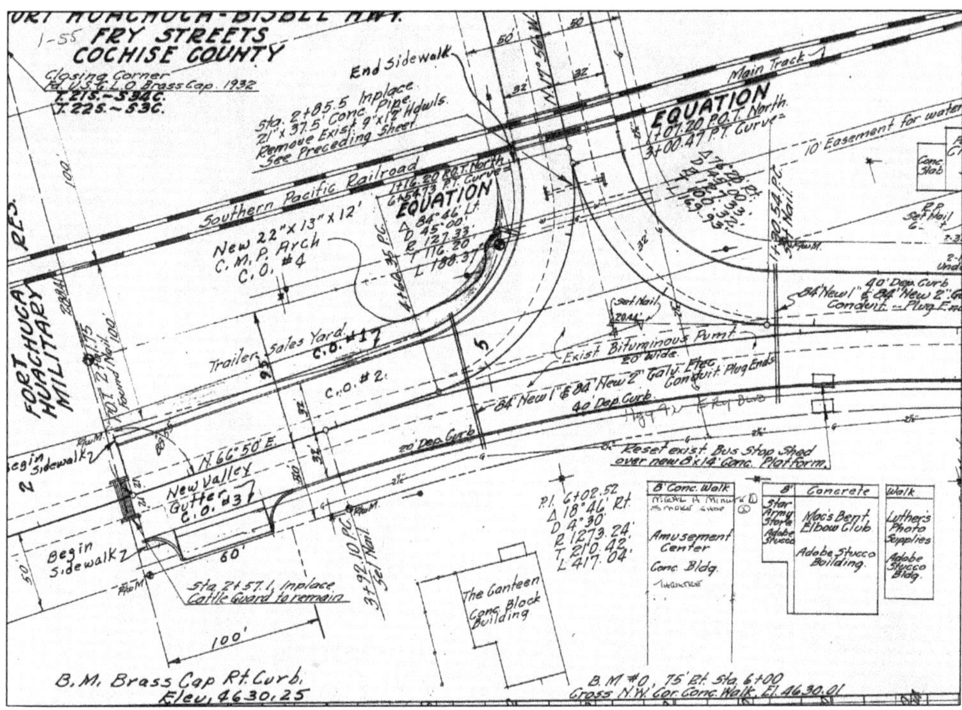

Number 3 in a set of six city street maps, annotated by K. Mayo. (Courtesy of Kathy Mayo and J. Herrewig.)

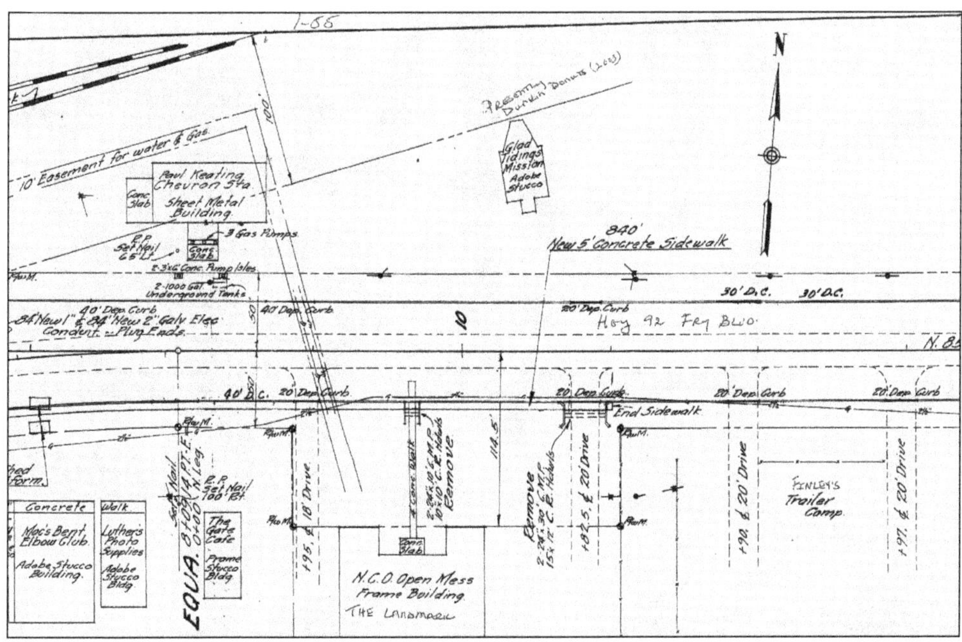

Number 4 in a set of six city street maps, annotated by K. Mayo. (Courtesy of Kathy Mayo and J. Herrewig.)

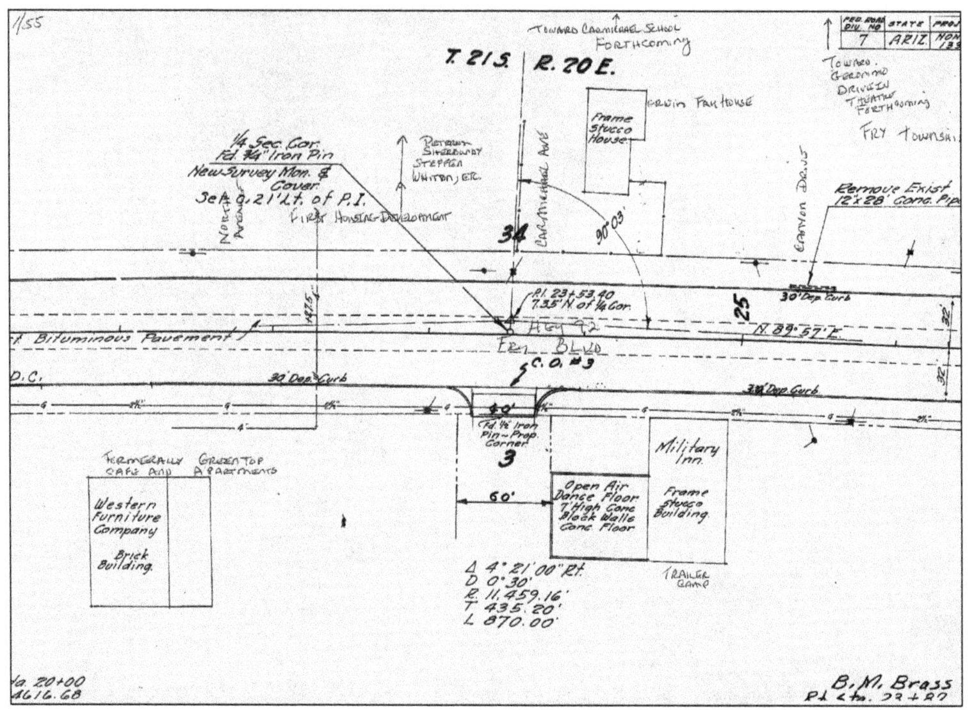

Number 5 in a set of six city street maps, annotated by K. Mayo. (Courtesy of Kathy Mayo and J. Herrewig.)

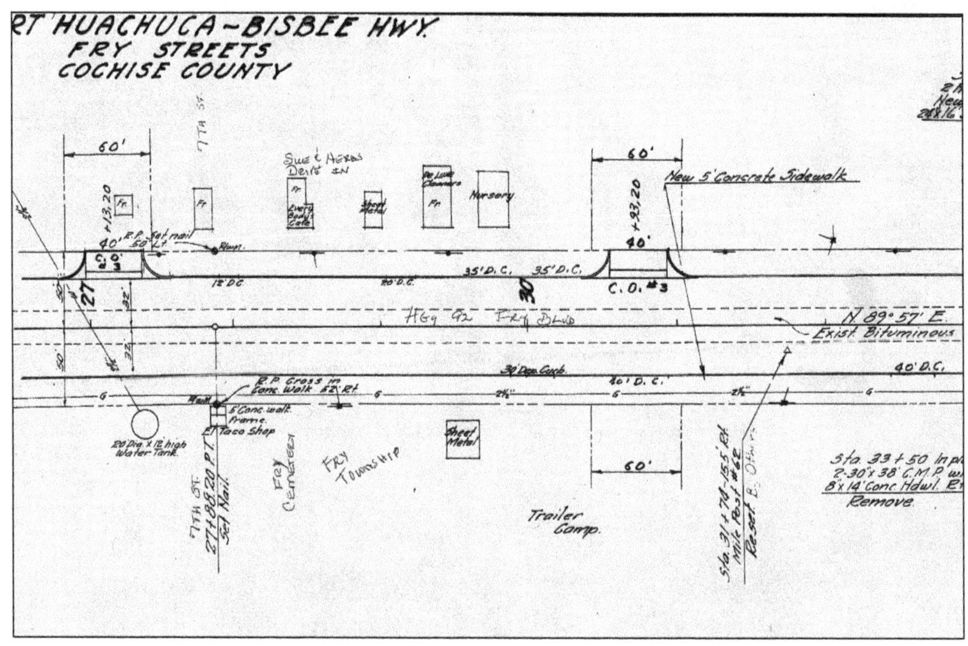

Number 6 in a set of six city street maps, annotated by K. Mayo. (Courtesy of Kathy Mayo and J. Herrewig.)

Appendix A: Names By Which Sierra Vista, and Parts Thereof, Has Been Known

Unknown dates: Hayes and Tanner Canyon

1878—Papingo: a card game; the name never really took hold, but it was used among some groups.

1898—Overton: source is obscure, but it has been suggested the name was that of a family living in the area.

1909—Garden Canyon: crops were grown by families living here, but the name was bestowed by the railroad bringing mail to the area.

1915—Buena: a name for the entire area; in 1915, it was usually mispronounced "B'yew-enna" or "Boo-enna." The word is Spanish, meaning "good."

1938—Fry: named for the prominent family who lived here because a small post office had been established in their home. It was the first "official" name for the community.

1942–1945—White City: named for a row of white buildings near the main gate to Fort Huachuca. The painted buildings housed "ladies of the night" until more such facilities were established along Fry Boulevard.

1942–1945—Hook: a name more in use by soldiers, this name refers to a specific business community along Fry Boulevard.

1955—Town of Sierra Vista: with incorporation, this was the Town of Sierra Vista, after several names were suggested and a vote taken.

1961—City of Sierra Vista: changed from the Town of Sierra Vista to the City of Sierra Vista, which it remains today.

Appendix B: Firsts

Mayor: R.W. Steffen

Female mayor: Ethel Berger, elected 1973 (Ms. Berger was also the first female mayor elected in the state of Arizona.)

City clerk: Marie Pfister (later Storment)

City attorney: Fred Talmadge

Police chief: Clarence Sherbundy

Building permit: Stanley Apartments, owned by Stanley Wenc

Commencement: Buena High School, May 26, 1959

Beauty contest: held in Sierra Vista in 1964 with winner Diane Gordon

Beer license: issued to Doc's Chicken Roost, August 28, 1956

Museum: Henry Hauser Historical Museum

Museum curator: Marisa Fusco

Bibliography

Books

Aleshire, Peter. *The Fox and the Whirlwind*. New York: John Wiley & Sons, 2000.

Alexander, David V. *Arizona Frontier Military Place Names 1846–1912*. Yucca Tree Press, 1998.

Altschuler, Constance Wynn. *Cavalry Yellow & Infantry Blue*. Tucson: The Arizona Historical Society, 1991.

Ball, Eve. *In the Days of Victorio*. Tucson: University of Arizona Press, 1970.

Campbell, Julie A., et al. *Studies in Arizona History*. Tucson: The Arizona Historical Society, 1998.

Cottrell, Marie G. *The Garden Canyon Project*. Tucson: Statistical Research, Inc., 1993.

Dickey, Norine Haverty, Mary Estes, ed. *Manzanita Cowboys and Twine Pasture Fences*. Phoenix: Huachuca Brand Press, 1999.

Faulk, Odie B. *The Geronimo Campaign*. New York: Oxford University Press, 1969.

Goff, John S. *Arizona Civilization*. Cave Creek, AZ: Black Mountain Press, 1974.

Gray, John Plesent. *When All Roads Led to Tombstone*. Ed. & Annotated by W. Lane Rogers. Boise, ID: Tamarack Books, 1998.

Hein, Jac. *Early Sierra Vista: Its People and Neighbors*. Sierra Vista: self-published, 1983.

Leckie, William H. *The Buffalo Soldiers*. Norman: The University of Oklahoma Press, 1967.

Martin, Douglas D. *An Arizona Chronology*. Tucson: University of Arizona Press, 1966.

Miller, Tom. *On the Border*. New York: Harper & Row, 1981.

Myrick, David F. *Railroads of Arizona: Vol. 1*. Berkeley, CA: Howell North Books, 1975.

Nearing, Richard and David Hoff. *Arizona Military Installations: 1752–1922*. Tempe, AZ: Gem Publishing, 1995.

Neuner, John D. *Arizona Myths, Fallacies, and Misconceptions*. Phoenix, AZ: First Leaf Publishing, 2001.

Pamachena, Ron. *The Border is Here.* Sierra Vista: Sycamore Research Services, 1993.

Public Sector Information. Arizona Yearbook 1997–1998. Eugene, OR: Public Sector Information, Inc.

Santor, David A. *The History of the Sierra Vista Police Department: 1956-1999.* Sierra Vista: self-published, *c.* 2000.

Shelton, Richard. *Going Back to Bisbee.* Tucson: University of Arizona Press, 1992.

Smith, Cornelius C. Jr. *Fort Huachuca: The Story of a Frontier Post.* Honolulu, HI: University Press of the Pacific, 1981, 2000.

Taylor, Leonard. *Hiker's Guide to the Huachuca Mountains.* Sierra Vista: Thunder Peak Productions, 1991.

———. *Discover the San Pedro Valley.* Sierra Vista: Agave Guides, 2000.

Trimble, Marshall. *Arizona—A Cavalcade of History.* Tucson, AZ: Treasure Chest Publications, 1989.

———. *Roadside History of Arizona.* Missoula, MT: Mountain Press Publishing, 1986.

Vanderpot, Rein and Teresita Majewski. *The Forgotten Soldiers.* Tucson, AZ: prepared for the Department of the Army at Fort Huachuca, AZ. Tech Series 71 Statistical Research, Inc., June 1998.

Wagoner, Jay J. *Early Arizona: Prehistory to Civil War.* Tucson: University of Arizona Press, 1975.

Walker, Henry P. and Don Bufkin. *Historical Atlas of Arizona, Second Edition.* Norman, OK: University of Oklahoma Press, 1979, 1986.

Newspapers

Tombstone Epitaph, April 1921–August 1921
Bisbee Daily Review, April 1921–August 1921
Huachuca Herald, October 1955–June 1956
Daily Herald-Dispatch, October 1964–November 1964
Daily Herald, June 1998–present

Video and audio taped oral histories sponsored by and maintained at the Henry Hauser Museum in Sierra Vista, Arizona.

Index

www.ingramcontent.com/pod-product-compliance
Lightning Source LLC
Chambersburg PA
CBHW050616110426
42813CB00008B/2582

* 9 7 8 1 5 8 9 7 3 0 6 5 6 *